THE

SUCCESS

RITUALS

Winning Habits of High-Achieving Women

VOLUME 2

Compiled by Gina Raelene

The Success Rituals:

Winning Habits of High-Achieving Women Volume 2

© 2020 Gina Raelene, Victress Press

Saskatchewan, Canada

thesuccessrituals.com

ISBN: 978-0-9866867-3-3

This book is dedicated to women in business

who add value and increase to the lives of others

by daring to do work they love.

Their success illuminates and expands

every woman's sense of possibility

through entrepreneurship.

INTRODUCTION

You know the uh-huh, mmm-hmm, or amen! you sometimes feel as you're reading another woman's story and discover that her opinion or experience mirrors your own?

That sense of connection, and common ground you feel as she validates you, substantiates your theories, teaches you or inspires you?

Books like The Success Rituals demonstrate how hungry we are for women leaders to share their stories and to impart their wisdom. Having published and contributed to numerous compilations like this, I know the impact of a single chapter can be deep and far-reaching.

I've been an entrepreneur in the online space since the end of 2006. And over the years I've come to love joint ventures, collaborations and multi-expert endeavours. They come in all shapes and sizes creating unique opportunities for those who come out to play to divide the effort and multiply the result.

Women entrepreneurs who have business girlfriends to play with rise to higher levels of success faster – and have more fun! Collaboration strategy (aka The Girlfriends Effect) will always be one of my favorite things to teach and to coordinate.

A book project takes collaboration to an exciting new level because good old-fashioned paper and ink is still the crème de la crème of written 'content'.

And writing (or contributing to) a book is one of the most effective ways to guide potential clients from INTERESTED in what you do to INVESTED to work with you. It showcases your work, creates a connection with the reader, starts a conversation and, when done well, confirms their hunch that you are exactly who they've been looking for.

I could go on to share all the reasons why I believe every woman entrepreneur should consider becoming an author (and there are many) but I'll summarize with this:

Writing a book, even a chapter in one, helps you to focus your work and to articulate your ideas clearly and concisely. Putting your ideas out there builds confidence and getting published builds authority.

"There's a certain amount of vulnerability, passion and drive that goes into writing a book. And when a female entrepreneur can tap into this, their writing not only helps their business but helps them build confidence around their unique message and mission," ~ Mona Patel CEO Motivate Design

These are just a few reasons why I created VICTRESS PRESS – the publishing arm of The Success Rituals series of books and a growing lineup of female authors. In fact, our debut author's book achieved International best-seller status before her official release!

A victress is a female achiever. It's my vibe. These are the women I love to work with and exactly who we have compiled this book for…the go-getters, the make-it-happeners, and those who want to be.

By placing the winning habits of high-achieving women under a spotlight, we will inspire you to become more aware of the things you think and do on a daily basis – exposing your success rituals, or lack of – so you can purposefully and positively influence your success too.

The stories inside this book are thought provoking reminders of the key ingredients that make a winning habit winning, consistent and intentional daily action. The reward for creating success rituals is new and extraordinary results in your business and life!

"Habits are first cobwebs, then cables." – Spanish proverb

As you read The Success Rituals Volume 2, you'll find chapters that seem written just for YOU. Pay close attention to them because I believe you've attracted this book into your life for a reason.

Are you ready to learn the winning habits of high-achieving women? Let's go…

Gina Raelene,

CEO, VICTRESS PRESS

GINA RAELENE

GINA RAELENE

WE WRITE - WE GROW

If you have a website, you are a publisher. If you are on social media, you are in marketing. And that means we are all writers. ~ Ann Handley, Author of Everybody Writes

As entrepreneurs in the online space, you probably already write every day. You write and respond to emails, post to social platforms, comment on other people's blogs and social media blurbs.

I want to encourage you to recognize these activities for what they are: writing. And, to consider them a legitimate and professional aspect of your daily routine.

Being able to communicate well in writing is an often overlooked and underleveraged cornerstone of attracting clients through content.

"Love is in the details" has been one of my mantras for years. And from this perspective you'll find that words matter far more than we give them credit for.

Words are one of the most powerful ways to convey what's important to your clients, customers and the world. Words are ambassadors for your personal brand and the common ground that starts conversations, ignites interest, stimulates desire and inspires action.

Rapport and trust are rarely established through clever marketing, and instead require that you learn to, and become willing to. speak genuinely from the heart.

Writing skills might vary from entrepreneur to entrepreneur, but the most successful among us all have two things in common: we make time to write regularly and we are purposeful with our words.

I have three ideas for you to consider for each one:

MAKE TIME TO WRITE REGULARLY

#1 Your Physical Writing Space

It's easier to stick to your daily writing habit when you want to spend time in the place where you write. You don't have to have a beautiful view or an expensive desk. Privacy and intention are more important than the quality of your surroundings. Maybe you prefer to stand while you work, or you feed off the energy of a bustling coffee shop. Do what you prefer and refine it as you go along.

Keep your inspiration, books, and research materials close at hand. Tape favorite quotes to your computer or a nearby wall. Keeping your space clean can also have a powerful effect on your determination. Work at this space at the same time every day for seven days in a row and pay attention to any changes you experience as you progress as well as distractions that arise.

One of the best pieces of advice I received around minimizing distractions is when writing, don't stop, not even to do a quick google search. Make a note in the text and follow up on it later. Take it a step further – close your web browser, turn off or mute social media notifications, put your phone on silent. Your best ideas will thank you for it.

Eventually you may find that habituating yourself with both a ritual time and place makes it easier to get into the zone when you start writing each day, and, while you're there, will make it easier to feel focused and stay inspired.

#2 Your Mental Writing Space

Many writers and entrepreneurs develop journaling routines to build self-confidence and harness creative potential. The Morning Pages exercise by Julie Cameron of The Artist's Way—where you write three pages every morning, by hand—is particularly useful for developing a solid writing habit. It can be about anything that pops into your head — and it's important that you get it all out of your head without editing or censoring in any way. No one has to read it (not even you), and it doesn't need to be magnificent.

Clearing away the cobwebs and creating space in your mind makes room for you to write the good stuff.

One final thought on this that honours the idea of a positive mental writing space is to consider creating content before consuming content. Inspiration is great but often, when I consume before I create my ideas are influenced in a way that dilutes my original intention or comparison creates doubt and delays. For me, this simple lens is a positive nuance of my writing habit.

As I consume, I do make notes of inspiration, areas of interest, quotes I love, references that might fuel future writing.

How you approach your writing habit can evolve and expand in ways that suit your style and support your success.

#3 Link to an Existing Habit

For example, I wake up, and before getting out of bed, I write in my gratitude journal which includes setting an intention for the day. Then, I make coffee and then, I begin to write. James Clear, author of Atomic Habits calls this having a cue. My cue is my cup of coffee. As you establish your writing habit (or other) through repetition, your body and mind will start to correlate your writing space, the time of day, the setting with "It's time to write."

An everyday example of this is flossing teeth. People who floss their teeth right after they brush their teeth are statistically more likely to make a habit of it. Flossing piggybacks brushing and over time it becomes a regular part of that morning routine.

Set aside writing time every single day, without exception. It's not about the duration it's about the routine. Your motivation will never be constant which is why your routine must be.

Be firm with yourself (and others) about your writing routine: the world will always try to tempt you away.

BE PURPOSEFUL WITH YOUR WORDS

#1 Use Emotion

As an entrepreneur, you can write and create content in a way that sounds factual (often boring unless you're Wikipedia), or you can write in a way that packs an emotional punch.

As you develop your writing ritual (routine & style), always aim to tug on the heartstrings of your reader.

Emotion makes your words memorable. People browse dozens if not hundreds of websites and social feeds every day. Most websites fail to draw their readers in emotionally. How many get you to laugh, get you to feel touched or get you to feel angry about something? How often do you feel like the content creator is talking directly to you, about your problems and that they understand where you're coming from?

Emotion makes your words remarkable. Shocking, funny and touching content that stirs up emotion gets shared and linked to a lot because they make people feel something, and that is memorable.

Emotion builds deeper relationships. Genuine, heart-felt content will help you build a much stronger bond with your readers.

People reading your content will feel like they can relate with you.

This translates to a livelier engaged community and helps to guide potential clients from interest to invested.

#2 Make It Personal

The single greatest enhancement you can make with your writing is practicing the skill of extracting value from your personal experiences and expressing the lessons learned.

Entrepreneurs who understand how to be genuine, emotional and relatable are the ones who win with their words.

People want to work with people they can relate to. People buy from people they trust. People gravitate toward people they share things in common with.

Your potential client wants to experience your writing/content the same way they would experience grabbing a cup of coffee with you at a local coffee shop.

They don't just want to know what you do, but how you do it. How did you first get into doing what you're doing now? How did you learn some of those early lessons? Did you have a mentor? What was he or she like? Did you always have this plan, or did it take a while for you to figure out what you wanted to do? Did you have any moments of failure? What were those like? How did you handle it?

#3 Pass the "So What?" Test

Whether you're writing a headline, a bio, an article or a chapter in a book, the "So what? Test" is a simple way to make sure you have your reader in mind and write what is relevant and interesting to them.

Your goal is to evaluate whether (or not) you are making a clear and significant claim that triggers an equally clear and bold conclusion from your ideal client.

Tip: Don't write about what you do, write about the ways people benefit from what you do.

Asking "So what?" leads you to write about benefits vs features, encourages you to back it up with proof and dramatically improves the purpose of your copy so that it grabs the reader's attention.

Bonus #4 Create Your Manifesto

One of my favorite ways my clients and I use words to create common ground with an audience is by creating a manifesto.

A manifesto is a declaration of principles, priorities and plans.

One of my favorite examples is from Lululemon. Commonly seen on their store bags, their manifesto has a fun visual bent. https://info.lululemon.com/about/our-story/manifesto

"Our manifesto is one way we share our culture with the community. It's an evolving collection of bold thoughts that allow for some real conversations to take place. Get to know our manifesto and learn more about what lights our fire."

Another basic example that most women can relate to is Oprah's "What I know for sure…" snippets in O Magazine.

Imagine doing the work you love for people who love you just the way you are… No competing, no comparing, just confidently declaring "This is me, this is what I do and this is how I can help you". That's the power of a manifesto.

You can get free access to my Create Your Manifesto masterclass here: http://manifesto.thesuccessrituals.com/

Ultimately, there are many ways an entrepreneur can benefit from developing a consistent and purpose-filled writing ritual -- You'll create opportunities to connect with potential clients in new and powerful ways and you'll inadvertently become a better writer too!

My final thought around this success ritual is:

Do you want to write more consistently and purposefully? And if yes, why?

Is it to start a blog, to build a following, to become known as a thought leader, to align your front-facing brand with your inner voice, to have a creative outlet, to write a book or to simply do a better job of guiding potential clients from interested in what you do to invested to work with you?

These are ALL great reasons. Which ones are most important to you? Your clarity and conviction around that will be a guiding force that keeps you on track when life's distractions try to steer you away.

ABOUT GINA RAELENE

Gina Raelene has inspired thousands of women entrepreneurs to expand what they believe is possible for them through entrepreneurship and the power of the internet.

She is the poster child of multi-passionate entrepreneur: Online Business Mentor and Success Catalyst to High-Achieving Women, CEO of Victress Press, Publisher of The Success Rituals series of books, and Co-Founder of BRAVE heR www.braveher.me.

Gina is a 6x best-selling author and has been published alongside industry legends like Brian Tracy and Bob Proctor of the hit movie The Secret. INFJ, Leo, Ravenclaw. Freedom is Gina's love language and entrepreneurship is one of her greatest passions (being a Nana is #1). If you're ready to achieve more online in record time, step inside Gina's world and buckle up buttercup!

To connect further make sure to subscribe to the BRAVE heR Morning Makeover 7-Day Mini Challenge at https://braveher.podia.com/brave-her-morning-makeover.

CARA WRAY

I MUST... I CAN'T... OH, BUT WHAT IF I CAN?

I used to feel like a hot mess Mama!

I used to wonder how so many other women looked like they had it all together. Balancing their business and babies, enjoying a successful relationship and living a thriving family life...

That life felt like it was so far out of reach for me. And I just couldn't wrap my mind around HOW they did it all.

I remember feeling anxious, annoyed and frustrated with my current reality. I felt like I was running on a never-ending hamster wheel and I was exhausted.

As I compared myself to other women, I worried wayyyy too much about what others thought of me. Can I just say, comparing yourself to Sally, Martha or Bernadette down the street will not do you any good. Comparison is NOT your friend. Comparison really is, as they say, a thief of joy and if you're struggling with it, I encourage you to tune back in - meaning get to know yourself again and fully EMBRACE her. Recognize everything you ARE doing and how amazing you are right NOW!

Unfortunately, my hot mess Mama moments included more than comparison.

I remember looking forward to FRIDAYS on Mondays and "living for the weekend" because I continuously overwhelmed myself with should do's, could do's and to do's.

I remember the feeling of "Mom Guilt" all too well. It actually kept me stuck for a long time. From one Mama to another - I think Mom Guilt is an excuse. It's an excuse that will keep you stuck and stagnant unless you make the conscious choice to reframe your mindset. Key word here: CHOICE.

What I've learned along this journey is:

I AM A PRIORITY. WHO I AM IS IMPORTANT. AND I MUST TAKE CARE OF MYSELF BEFORE I CAN FULLY TAKE CARE OF ANYONE ELSE.

It's time to choose you Mama. And I'm here to help you.

First things first, put yourself back onto your priorities list - right at the tippy-top! Stop treating yourself like a second or third or not an option. You deserve more than that. And I know you wouldn't want your children or spouse to treat themselves as low priority, so remember that the next time you push your own priorities to the side.

Next, I want to make sure you understand that your thoughts become your reality. So you need to open your eyes to your current reality and recognize that you have the power of choice. You get to shift your thinking -

and your reality - and you can do that in an instant. Be clear on what you want and then TAKE ACTION! Don't wait for opportunities to pass you by!

Last thought on this before we dive into addressing limiting beliefs that could get in your way... Your significant other and your children will thank you and appreciate the positive ripple effect that comes from placing your needs at the top of your list. They meet you at the level you treat yourself. You lead. You set the example.

Now, let's talk about those nitty gritty limiting beliefs that have been holding you back for FAR TOO LONG!

A limiting belief is a false belief that a person acquired as a result of making an incorrect conclusion about something in life. This can simply be something that your parents believed to be true while you were growing up that YOU then chose to believe as well. Example: "You have to go to post secondary to be successful". <- Limiting belief right there.

I truly hold space for each one of you to bring your goals, dreams and desires into fruition. I do for many reasons and it's truly time we open up this conversation. We can be our own worst enemy, our own worst critic and we hold the power and choice to silence the limiting beliefs that aren't serving our highest good.

I want you to know you are not alone. Your feelings are valid. Your emotions are meant to be felt and acknowledged. This is an extremely important step - ACKNOWLEDGEMENT! You cannot change what you turn a blind eye to.

Has anyone ever questioned the choices you've made for yourself? Whether it came down to choosing post-secondary, building a family, creating a business, your relationship and the list continues on.

Have you ever had someone impose their beliefs onto you? Meaning they believed their belief so strongly that they had an expectation for YOU to believe it too?

Have you ever sat with yourself and asked yourself - What do I ACTUALLY value most in this life? Have I conformed to fit the mold of others. Have I subconsciously held myself back? Have I remained comfortable to fit in or keep others comfortable too? Out of fear of rejection? These are all powerful questions to ask yourself.

I need to remind you that every action has a reaction and guess what - you hold that power of choice and it's time to take radical responsibility and start taking action towards the life you DESIRE to live. Ya with me?

Has anyone ever asked you these questions or said these statements to you:

What do you even do?

You're just a stay at home mom...

How is this sustainable?

You left a career to stay home with your children?

How are you supporting your family?

The debt you guys have must be weighing on you guys...

You hired a Coach to help you do what?

Why would you do something like that?

If I were you I would... (fill in the blank with unsolicited advice).

I've been asked many of these questions and they break my heart.

As a society we have allowed others to make decisions for us. Today I personally choose NOT to live this way, however - there was a time when I placed more value on the opinions of others rather than my own. I'm proud to be an entrepreneur, balancing my business alongside my babies and taking care of our home. I'm proud that I continue to push towards my dreams, goals and desires.

I believe that it's time, as a collective, that we take responsibility for what we ACTUALLY want. It's time we speak up about it. It's time we have the "tough" conversations. It's time we RISE and become the woman we were always meant to be.

This takes awareness, this takes accountability, this takes action, this takes commitment, this takes grace and this takes compassion.

Most of all this takes you choosing you!

And, this also requires you to fully deal with your shit. Yeah, the stuff you've suppressed for far too long because society told you that you had to and you believed it.

It's time to call BS on everything that does not serve your highest good. It's time to own your worth. It's time to take RADICAL responsibility for your life. You made choices that landed you right where you are now. And for some of you that's a tough pill to swallow.

Entrepreneurship places a magnifying glass on the thing you might not want to deal with but honey you gotta. Trust me. The work, the most beautiful work will always be the work you do on yourself and for yourself.

This leads me back to power and strength in self-prioritization. There should be ZERO guilt around placing your needs first.

Society has taught us to give until we feel lost, overwhelmed and depleted. We even hear people saying they LOVE the hustle. They LOVE to be constantly "doing". I call total BS. We as humans have been placed on planet earth to explore, learn, educate, expand, adventure, grow, love and expand. We were never made to conform and do things that don't serve our highest good and NO we were never meant to constantly HUSTLE.

If you've questioned how others have been able to balance it all, it really does start with you asking yourself the questions that shine a light on our shadows...sometimes the deepest parts of ourselves that we've suppressed.

How you see yourself.

The love you give to yourself.

How you speak to yourself.

How you speak to others.

It all matters.

YOU. GO. FIRST. - THE. UNIVERSE. RESPONDS.

So, I want to encourage you to take a good long look in the mirror and get clear about - what you really need?

We must be our first priority.

Because in doing so, we teach others and give them permission to make themselves a priority too.

Before we part ways and you move onto another awesome chapter in this book I want to guide you through a simple yet powerful exercise to help you identify any LIMITING BELIEFS that may be holding you back from making yourself a priority and living the life you so deeply desire.

HOW TO IDENTIFY A LIMITING BELIEF EXERCISE:

1. Grab a journal or paper. You will also need a pen or pencil. (Whatever your preference)

2. Ask yourself this question: What area of my life is currently making me feel unhappy,

disappointed, frustrated and or dissatisfied?

3. This is an important step - Ask yourself WHY?! Really dive deep into what is triggering you. (Lack of value/boundary, guilt?)

4. Within your why - you can now identify your limiting belief or a limiting belief of someone else that has projected onto you. (i.e. I can't, I'll try, what if, it's too good to be true)

5. Now, it's time to flip the script. List a minimum of 3 truths that break through your limiting belief. What do you know to be true beyond a shadow of a doubt? (shift the statements to I can, I will, I deserve, I desire)

It's important that you know you are deserving of an abundant life and as many say "abundance is your birthright".

Your strongest beliefs become your reality.

Take your power back, shift your perspective and choose what you believe because your strongest beliefs become your reality and you can create a reality that you love!

ABOUT CARA WRAY:

Cara Wray is a MULTI-PASSIONATE entrepreneur, author, podcast host and Co-Founder of BRAVE heR!

She is a wife, mother & step-mother to 4 beautiful children who believes your strongest beliefs become your reality.

To connect further make sure to subscribe to the BRAVE heR Morning Makeover 7-Day Mini Challenge at: morning.braveher.me.

VICTORIA WELSH

THE GIFTS OF GRATITUDE ARE GRAND

At the beginning of April 2020, my son Brayden and I lost our home and a great deal of our possessions to flood and mold. The tragedy was compounded by the fact that we were still in mourning over losing my beloved Mama just 2 weeks prior.

It was a very trying time for us.

And through it ALL - we stayed grounded in GRATITUDE!

Gratitude for the unknown

Gratitude for the known

Gratitude for what was

Gratitude for what was to come

Gratitude for the certainty

Gratitude for the uncertainty

When I would wake in the morning with my breath taken away by the realization of my reality, I would immediately tap into gratitude for everyone being safe!

When I would go to bed at night and I wanted to reach for the phone and call my Mom and my emotion shifted to sadness, I would tap into gratitude for all the memories and beautiful times we shared.

When I would think of the overwhelming job ahead of me, I would tap into gratitude that I was physically capable of moving myself, that I worked for myself and could take the time I needed, that Brayden was being homeschooled and wasn't missing school due to our situation.

There are ALWAYS things to be grateful for - even when you are going through the biggest storms of your life.

Gratitude shifts your vibrational frequency and opens up channels for you to receive GIFTS FROM SOURCE!

We can't see what is coming for us! And we don't know the plans of GOD/Universe.

Your ONLY job is to make sure you are a vibrational energetic match for the GIFTS!

The gifts of gratitude are grand and I'm living proof.

I have had a Beach Bungalow/Cottage on my vision board since 2011.

On April 23, 2020 we moved into an adorable yellow Bungalow directly across from the beach - a home that is on what was once Native American sacred ground with an Artesian Well that runs directly under the ground in Indian Rocks Beach, Florida.

My greatest success ritual is having a daily practice of gratitude. And, when the storms of life come I tap into GRATITUDE even deeper!

Through gratitude gifts and blessings come - IF - you are in alignment, energetically, to receive them!

When you have gratitude for what you already have in your life, it opens you up energetically to receive more! The Law of Attraction works in this way 100% of the time!

Gratitude elevates your energetic frequency. It is the HOLY GRAIL of manifestation! But, it's not all spiritual woo. You'll find proof in scientific studies too!

Practicing gratitude can affect your brain and heart in the most profound ways.

According to UCLA's Mindfulness Awareness Research Center:

Having an attitude of gratitude changes the molecular structure of the brain, keeps gray matter functioning, and makes us healthier and happier. When you FEEL happiness, the central nervous system is affected. You are more peaceful, less reactive and less resistant. Now that's a really cool way of taking care of your well-being.

Emotions and other factors associated with consciousness have the power to transform our inner world in ways we don't fully understand yet. These findings show how consciousness can actually transform the physical/material world, and that's huge. This validates the idea that if we can change our inner world through gratitude, empathy, compassion, and meditation, we can make our outer world more peaceful.

To put it simply… gratitude is the gateway to JOY. Practicing gratitude helps to clear away negative emotional baggage that blocks your natural state of abundance and your ability to manifest your heart's desires.

Now that you know WHY gratitude is so darned important, let's look at HOW you can embody a daily practice of gratitude.

For years now, I have practiced the Art of Gratitude several times daily. The first method I practice as soon as I wake in the morning, the second method I apply throughout the day as I receive gifts/manifestations from God/Source/Creator and lastly, I developed an intentional daily practice of what I referred to as "manifesting gratitude". I will share the details of all three practices with you below.

I feel it is very important to acknowledge that these daily practices raised my baseline vibe or 'emotional set point' from one of contentment to one of pure enthusiasm and joy. You can find more information about your Emotional set point in the book "Ask and It Is Given" by Esther and Jerry Hicks.

I was going through a dark night of my soul when I learned about the practice of Gratitude and its many benefits on health. At the time, I was suffering from insomnia, depression and panic attacks. I was looking for alternative methods, a more holistic approach, to my conditions. I was introduced to yoga and meditation and during my research, I stumbled upon the practice of gratitude and its scientifically proven results on health, including better sleep, increased energy and vitality, and decreased depression and anxiety. I had nothing to lose and everything to gain.

Be forewarned, your life may change for the absolute betterment when you apply an intentional daily practice of Gratitude. I personally have no more depression or anxiety, amazing sleep and I have become more productive, more successful and have manifested more Abundance than ever from my "Attitude of Gratitude".

I feel it is important to note here that there is a difference between being thankful and expressing gratitude. Being thankful is something we tend to do spontaneously when someone helps us or does something for us, like holding the door for us. We say "thank you". It is an acknowledgment of thanks for something someone has given you or done for you. Thankfulness is usually fleeting.

Gratitude is more of an embodiment. It's a feeling throughout your entire being. It's an emotion expressed in appreciation for the goodness in your life. The appreciation is felt in the depths of you. It's a response to something that has had an impact on your life. It is a practice that can be cultivated, and it grows over time. Your life can and will expand as your gratitude practice expands.

Over time and with practice, you will become the embodiment of Gratitude. You will no longer have to intentionally practice gratitude; it will become a part of who you are!

Additionally, as your practice of Gratitude grows, you will raise your emotional set point and as y0u raise your emotional set point, you raise your vibrational frequency which makes you an energetic match for more greatness. When you raise your vibe, you begin to attract things into your life that are on the same vibrational frequency. This is the Law of Attraction at work.

1. WAKING UP WITH AN ATTITUDE OF GRATITUDE:

I have a catchphrase in my online coaching practice. I do a daily Livestream for my audience and I finish each Livestream with the same catchphrase: "Remember to wake up tomorrow with an Attitude of Gratitude and say 5 things you are grateful for the second your feet hit the floor in the morning".

I say this catch phrase because gratitude is that powerful. The practice of Gratitude changed my life so significantly and it was such a simple shift into this practice that my wish is for everyone to be able to embrace a daily practice of gratitude and raise their vibrational frequency. My intention is for you to raise your emotional set point to one of joy, appreciation, freedom!

Starting your day with gratitude raises your vibrational frequency and starts your day in a high vibe. Practice embodying gratitude as soon as you open your eyes in the morning or as soon as your feet hit the floor. Whichever time you choose, just make it specific and keep it consistent so that when you do the thing (open your eyes or place your feet on the floor) your brain will be triggered to begin the practice of gratitude and this will become something you won't even have to think about, rather an embodiment for you.

There are several avenues in which you can express this gratitude such as, you may wish to keep a gratitude journal next to your bed and write down 5 things you are grateful for upon awakening or you may have someone in particular in mind and you want to write them a short note of gratitude or you could just say the 5 things you are grateful for - speak them out loud (or in your mind).

Begin to think about what you are grateful for right now in your life. This could be people (your loved ones, family, children, partner, your employees, your supportive friends, your helpful co-workers) or things you have attained/manifested (your home, your vehicle, your cozy sofa, your patio furniture) or things in nature that bring you joy (the sunshine, the clouds, the sound of rain, the beach, a mountain side, the forest) or things you enjoy doing (hiking, painting, swimming, biking, having a beach day with girlfriends, spa treatments).

Just know that your gratitude does not have to be of grandiose and outrageous substance. Sometimes my morning gratitude looks like this: I am so grateful and thankful for my morning cup of coffee, the sunshine beaming in my window, the feeling of the breeze on my face, the big white puffy clouds in the sky and for getting a good night's sleep in my cozy bed.

There are ALWAYS things to be grateful for. We overlook these simple pleasures in life because we get so busy with our day to day activities.

Gratitude helps you to slow down for a moment and recognize that which you currently have but may inadvertently be overlooking due to the hustle and bustle of your daily life.

No matter HOW you choose to express your gratitude, the KEY to The Art of Gratitude is to FEEL the appreciation in your body when you are expressing the things you are grateful for.

It is not enough to just say or write down 5 things you are grateful for and recall them in your mind. It is imperative that you FEEL the emotion of appreciation in your body as you speak or write out your gratitude. This is the embodiment practice of Gratitude.

This would look like this: I would speak "I am so grateful for my morning cup of coffee". I would then recall in my mind's eye what it looks like when I'm holding my morning cup of coffee, how I hold the mug, how warm it feels in my hands, how I smell my coffee first, inhaling it's intoxicating aroma and then taking that first sip that is oh so satisfying. A smile would then come over my face as I feel the feeling of appreciation in my body for my morning cup of coffee. I then take a deep breath and continue to feel the appreciation throughout my entire being, as I can feel my vibe rising by just feeling gratitude for my morning coffee.

I continue on with the 4 other things that I feel gratitude for and each time I feel the feeling of appreciation in my body, I am stacking that feeling on top of the appreciation I just felt, allowing the gratitude stack to grow bigger and bigger. Each time feeling deeper and deeper appreciation, until I am beaming with joy! This is what I refer to as "growing my vibe".

Do the embodiment practice whether you speak or write your gratitude. The embodiment is the most indispensable component of this practice.

Continue this daily intentional practice of morning gratitude until you no longer have to think about doing it, it just becomes a part of who you are.

Waking up with an "attitude of Gratitude" cultivates an attitude of gratitude throughout your day. Additionally, it is a habit you can develop which will serve you very well during the challenging times of your life. By building your gratitude muscles, you are able to tap into this frequency when you are going through a difficult time.

This is how I was able to stay balanced and peaceful during the most challenging time of my adult life when I lost my mother and just 2 weeks later, lost my home and all that I owned. I intentionally applied gratitude for the things that I found gratitude for, despite what I was going through. This is how I can say that I know there are always things you can find gratitude for.

2. CELEBRATION of GRATITUDE

The second practice of gratitude that I apply in my daily life is what I call "celebration gratitude".

It is scientifically based that happiness helps people be more successful, just as gratitude helps people to be happier. Therefore, the more gratitude you practice, the happier you become.

A celebration of gratitude is a celebration of appreciation in the moment for something that you have just manifested into your life, something that has just shown up. You may have been intentionally manifesting it or not. It may or may not have been one of your goals. We generally celebrate something arriving that we have been praying for or something we have been taking action towards. However, we overlook life's unexpected manifestations and we don't give them much attention. So, in respect to the Celebration of Gratitude, I am speaking more to the unexpected that shows up in your life.

We are always manifesting. It's the Universal Law of Attraction in action. Sometimes we intentionally manifest and other times we just call things into our awareness. The surprises that life brings us are something that we have to be a vibrational match in order to receive. The exciting thing about the little surprises is knowing that you are an energetic match to receive it which gives us evidence that we are raising that emotional set point. The more we raise our vibe, the more exciting surprises show up. Or perhaps we just notice them and appreciate them more as we focus our attention on them. Either way, it's a win!

When these manifestations show up, I celebrate them in many different ways; sometimes with an appreciation dance, sometimes I excitedly declare what I just manifested and say "Thank you God/Source/Creator". Other times, I call a friend so we can celebrate together with our screeches of excitement. When I find coins on the ground, I pick them up and kiss them and hold them in the air and shriek: "Thank you Universe. I am a good receiver. I'll take more please". I have a jar of parking lot coins at home that says "Gifts from God" on the label. It's a reminder that I am always being gifted!

We must learn to be good receivers and acknowledge and celebrate the gifts bestowed upon us. Whether it's a free coffee at your favorite coffee shop, a free bagel with purchase of a drink, or pennies found in the parking lot, these are all gifts from the Universe and the Universe likes to give to good receivers.

Adding celebration of gratitude to your repertoire raises your vibrational frequency, shows the Universe you are a good receiver, and increases your happiness.

3. MANIFESTING GRATITUDE

The final gratitude tool that I implement in my day to day life centers around intentional manifestation. These are the clients, the abundance, the material things (new home, new car) that I am currently calling into my life. This manifestation technique works for everything you are desiring to materialize into your reality.

It's important to create a daily time or event in your day that will trigger y0u to remember to actually implement this practice, as this practice relies on your daily attention to your vision of your future. The time I choose each day to integrate this practice into my life is when I take a shower. It gives me just the amount of time that I enjoy spending forward focused on my vision for my life!

This is a simple practice, but you must know what you desire first.

Know your desires then create a clear vision of those desires. As y0u develop this clear vision in your mind's eye, then you can engage in a practice of giving gratitude for this very thing you desire.

Manifesting gratitude is giving gratitude for the very thing you are intentionally manifesting into your life. See the vision of your desire in your mind's eye. Hold the vision while simultaneously feeling in your body what it will feel like to have this thing. Feel the excitement in your body, feel the appreciation all throughout your body for having manifested this into your life. Now state your appreciation out loud. Speak it into existence. Such as… "I am so grateful and thankful for the abundance in my life. I am so grateful to have reached consistent $10K cash months in my business. It feels so amazing to have this financial abundance and freedom in my life."

Set aside time to do this practice every single day and you will begin to see y0ur desires manifest into your reality.

Now it's your turn. I shared with you 3 ways that I personally practice and integrate Gratitude into my day to day life. If you're ready to start manifesting at light speed, open yourself up to new opportunities and become a master receiver choose one of these practices and be intentional as you integrate the wonders of Gratitude into your life.

For more information on gratitude and manifestation, I invite you to join my FREE Facebook community for women at where y0u can participate in a 10 day Gratitude challenge that will improve y0ur manifestation game and raise your vibrational frequency.

ABOUT VICTORIA WELSH

Victoria is an Intuitive Women's Empowerment + Success Coach. She helps women to heal emotional wounds, build confidence, awaken to their purpose, and activate the Divine Feminine within in order to increase abundance and wealth in their lives with ease and flow.

She is mother to 2 incredible children, Brianna and Brayden, and Vivie to her amazing granddaughter, Nova Lynne.

She is known to do big BOLD things. She left her comfy nursing career of 24 years to follow her dreams and founded the brand The Fierce Feminine. She believes EVERY woman should know how magical she is and how much she is supported by God/Source/Creator.

You can find her hanging out on Facebook and Instagram @thefiercefemininecoach or in The Fierce Feminine Sisterhood Facebook Group.

STEPHANIE POLLOCK

ONE RITUAL TO RULE THEM ALL

"Do we want to stay a high-impact boutique business, or do we want to grow into a much bigger company?"

This was the question on the table; the one I'd been asked to come in and help facilitate between two ambitious, smart women. They were at a crossroads in their company and were keen to make some strategic decisions about their future and what they were building. At the core was a question most entrepreneurs come to at some point - do we stay, or do we grow?

Their company had already gone through several changes over the years by the time we gathered for a full-day day session in one of their living rooms on a crisp fall day.

One of the original business partners had recently exited the company, the other had weathered the storm of burnout, and now a new business partner had stepped in, bringing fresh energy and ideas to the table. Quickly they were gaining traction and clients were coming onboard with relative ease.

And yet, something was nagging at them both.

They instinctively knew that they were at a key decision point - one that would direct how they moved forward, what mix of clients they took on and what kind of business they were about to build.

Exponential growth was a very real option but with it would come with its own challenges - namely, their deep desire for a life outside of work. Still, opportunity was knocking and the idea of turning work down seemed absurd. Isn't growth what every entrepreneur dreams of? Could they say no to the big-fish clients that would likely come their way? Were they crazy to consider a different way?

They hired me to facilitate a session to help them make a decision they could feel confident about. Our focus was clear: refresh the company's values to reflect their new partnership and use these values to decide how they would lead the company and their clients.

Fast-forward eight hours, many cups of coffee and dozens of sticky-notes up all over the walls, they came to one piercing point of clarity; they would stay a small-but-mighty boutique company focused on impact and inspiration. They would be incredibly discerning about the clients they took on, opting for a business structure that allowed for time with family, Friday's off and project work where they could create lasting value. And it was their values work that showed them the way forward.

Today, more than seven years later, they are still going strong and staying true to the values we established. Despite market changes, client challenges and personal goals, these partners have circled back to their values again and again to keep them connected to what matters most. Their values have kept them grounded, focused and confident throughout it all.

Values are the ultimate success ritual.

Despite what a critical role values play, unfortunately few entrepreneurs leverage this foundational part of building a business. They bypass values work for the sexy stuff: sales funnels, fancy logos, webinars, automation, social media and whatever else is bright and shiny. Or, they say they'll get around to it one day - once the clients come in, once the money is in their bank account, once they've established themselves in the marketplace.

But this is a backward approach. Instead, establishing your company's values should be at the very top of your priority list.

Values might not be sexy or shiny, but they'll offer you something that most business-building strategies never can: long-term clarity, confidence and connection regardless of how your business evolves, the market changes or the world gets disrupted (exhibit: COVID-19).

Build a values-led business

Before we go further, let's establish a working understanding of what values are - specifically as it relates to your business (you'll want to have a set of personal values that inform and align with your company values too).

Values: a core belief that signifies what matters most, informs what actions and decisions to make, and creates a shared culture and commitment.

Values operate as guideposts to help you make informed decisions, face uncertainty and ambiguity, and take strategic action in pursuit of your greater vision. And values serve as internal motivators - it's what fuels your fire and keeps you going, even when things get hard (and it always does).

Values are not morals, they are not rules, they are not principles, they are not things that you have or do (money is not a value), they are not activities (travelling is not a value) and they are not based on should-dos. When your business has vague, unclear values (or no established values at all), you're likely to see a few things going on, including:

Loose boundaries

Clients that aren't good fits

Compromising (payments, pricing, deadlines etc.)

Doing work that isn't aligned with what's important to you

Burnout, exhaustion, frustration

Poor decision-making

Conflict (or conflict avoidance)

How values help shape your company's culture

Operating a business - whether as a company of one or one hundred - is an active, people-centric process. There are many moving parts that all play a pivotal role in the success of your company, from marketing to sales to customer service to business development to team building to strategic planning. As the leader of your business, you've likely made a million different decisions about all of these areas and more.

But the bigger question is: what informed these decisions?

When you've done the work to figure out our company values, decision-making gets a whole lot clearer. Notice I didn't say easier, because many decisions in business require deep thought and careful consideration. But knowing your values - what you stand for and what's most important - brings the answers into focus in a way that nothing else can. Often, you'll have to make a hard call because of it, but you'll do so knowing you haven't compromised what matters most.

Establishing clear values will help you in every aspect of business-building, especially as you work to embed them across functions and teams. They'll help you highlight and celebrate your best efforts and they'll serve as a guide when business throws you a curveball. And they'll also serve as warning signals, letting you know when you've gone off course or are about to step into territory you have no business stepping in.

As you can see, values permeate all areas of your business, which is why putting attention here is one of the best business investments you'll ever make.

Let's get started!

There are three steps to building a values-based business:

Uncover and name your company values

Build a practice of leading from them everyday

Commit to staying accountable to your values

1. Uncover and identify your company values

Google "company values" and you'll find a slew of posts with lists of words like, "Integrity, boldness, honesty, learning and community." Most will ask you to choose from this laundry-list of words based on what resonates most.

The problem with this approach, which I call "shopping for values," is that they're often chosen based on what we believe we should value. What company doesn't value honesty or integrity, right? This impersonal way of cherry-picking values may seem fine at first, but when rubber hits the road, they'll prove themselves somewhat meaningless and ambiguous.

Instead, deciding on your company values should be a thoughtful exercise based on much more than a commonplace set of words. Values are deeply personal, action-oriented commitments your business will make. They should reflect your personality, your purpose, your worldview and your convictions.

Uncovering your values takes time and effort, and should be done in collaboration with your team (who will be charged with living and leading from them).

Here are a few questions to get you started as you either define or refresh your values:

What are we willing to stand for - even if it ruffles a few feathers?

What do we want our customers, clients and the community to say about us behind our backs?

What are our non-negotiables? Where are we unwilling to ever compromise?

What actions and ways-of-being are we absolutely, unequivocally committed to above all else?

2. Build a practice of leading from your values every day

Walk into any major company, and you're likely to see a list of values on a glass plaque in the lobby or reception area. Scan an annual report, scroll through a major brand's website or listen to a Fortune 500 CEO deliver a speech, and you're likely to learn what their company values are.

But a list of words is simply that - a list of words. And people - namely your potential customers and clients - see through lip-service pretty quickly. Chances are good, if you were to think of a company that frustrates you or has left you feeling disappointed, you'll be able to pinpoint the issue to a values disconnect. They may say "customer service" is really important but when you have to make 15 calls just to get the right package delivered, you recognize that those words mean nothing in practice.

Leadership is a practice, not a position.

Values are inherently meaningless if you aren't practicing them and leading from them every day. This step requires a bias toward action, however messy it may be along the way. It's time to put your values into action. It's easy to declare what you believe - anyone can do that - but it's much harder and much more meaningful to demonstrate those words in the ways you conduct yourself each and every day. This is the hard part, and the biggest opportunity for impact and distinction.

As you consider where to apply and embed your values, think of:

- Your strategic planning process: how can your values inform your path ahead and where you put your focus?
- Your HR process: how do your values help you making hiring, firing, performance reviews, expectation-setting and team-building decisions?
- Your marketing: how do you communicate your values through your content, your speaking and your promotions?
- Your offers: how can your values help you determine what services, products or programs to create and what outcomes you want to achieve?

- Your culture: how will your values create a shared language, shape your team culture and give everyone a clear vision for the future?

3. Commit to a values accountability-framework

Once you've identified your values and begun to embed them into the way you operate, your final step is to build an accountability framework to ensure you stay true to what you say.

The unfortunate truth is that many companies are quick to come up with a list of values, but are hesitant to be accountable to them when presented with a challenging situation. This is a big mistake and one that will likely cost you customers and your credibility.

Never has this become more clear than in recent months as our global community wrestles with COVID19 and racial discrimination and unrest. These are big issues that impact us all in markedly different ways, and for many businesses, they've become a lightning rod for anger, resentment and cancel culture.

At the core of it all is usually one main issue: the company says they value one thing but their actions suggest another. And then, when they're called out for this inconsistency, they avoid, deflect or defend rather than take ownership, or they scramble to say they care in a way that rings hollow with their audience.

Conversely, companies that have already committed to values work and are actively leading, operating and communicating from those values stand out from the crowd and draw new business as people seek out brands that walk their talk. People trust them to do the right thing and to operate with integrity.

As the wise Brené Brown says,

"One reason we roll our eyes when people start talking about values is that everyone talks a big values game but very few people actually practice one. It can be infuriating, and it's not just individuals who fall short of the talk. In our experience, only about 10 percent of organizations have operationalized their values into teachable and observable behaviors that are used to train their employees and hold people accountable. Ten percent. If you're not going to take the time to translate values from ideals to behaviors—if you're not going to teach people the skills they need to show up in a way that's aligned with those values and then create a culture in which you hold one another accountable for staying aligned with the values—it's better not to profess any values at all. They become a joke. A cat poster. Total BS."

Here are a few ideas to bake accountability into your values process:

Tie values with performance by linking employee outcomes to specific values

Create a values scorecard to filter client opportunities

Create a bi-annual process with your team to review how well the company has lived into your values

Taking the time to go through these three steps will be one of the most clarifying and rewarding experiences of your entrepreneurial journey. You'll make better decisions, create stronger teams, feel more focused, hold better boundaries and provide a customer experience that people will remember (in a good way!).

Identify them, lead from them and stay true to them. Your values are like a lighthouse in the storm - showing you the safe way back home.

And in our ever-changing, volatile business environment, this will be your ultimate success ritual - the one you will turn to each and every day.

ABOUT STEPHANIE POLLOCK

Stephanie Pollock is a Leadership Coach, Host of the Lead Well podcast, writer and speaker. She's proudly Canadian and highly caffeinated.

She's also the founder of LEAD.Well - a monthly subscription to help women become better, braver leaders. Each month, we explore a new leadership theme through curated resources, a private member podcast, Leadership Lab workshops, Leader Retreats and a Book Club.

Success Rituals readers can take advantage of a special 30-day free trial of LEAD.Well by using the code: SUCCESSBOOK at weleadwell.co/successrituals.

AMY DEAGLE

BE BOLD

"Sometimes all you need is 20 seconds of insane courage … just 20 seconds of embarrassing bravery, and I promise you, something great will come of it." ~ We Bought a Zoo (2011)

I don't recall watching "We Bought a Zoo'; but that one line, uttered by Matt Damon's character to his son, has stayed with me since the moment I first heard it.

Looking back on my life, it is clear to me that these "20 seconds of insane courage" moments are the moments that make up our lives. It's in the opportunities to let life pass us by, or to rise up and claim our destiny that our lives are shaped and transformed, forever.

Each one of us has been put on this earth for a reason, a God-given purpose that is ours to fulfil. Unfortunately, there is no roadmap that accompanies us on this journey through life, and too many of us have simply put life into autopilot. Our decisions have become about convenience and instant gratification. The temptation to compare ourselves to others highlight reels, while we are stuck in our 'behind the scenes' and messy middles, cause us to give up on our hopes and dreams before we ever truly give them a chance to make their mark on the world.

These moments of courage are not a once in a lifetime opportunity. They are around us every day, and we are missing them because we are sleepwalking through life. We become so comfortable, complacent, and content with "good enough", that we miss out on the chance at great, extraordinary, passion-fueled purpose-driven lives.

How many of you have had that voice come up at one point or another in your life? It's usually some version of "who do you think you are", "what will "they" think", "what makes you so special", or "there's someone way more qualified than you, why even try". These inner thoughts sabotage us before we even get the idea out of our mouths. As quickly as these stirrings towards "more" come up, they can be shot down by your inner saboteur.

Applying for that job. Moving. Asking that person out. Switching careers. Leaving an "ok" relationship. Making new friends. Starting a business. Asking to be mentored.

All these things have the potential to change your life for the better, and they all have one thing in common; they require courage in action.

I can think of a handful of courageous moments that shaped by life into what it is today:

Standing under the arch at the University of Calgary at 18 years old, deciding if I should just move home and find someone to marry me, or stay and pursue a career in nursing, my childhood dream

Sitting on a plane, bound for Sitka, Alaska at 23 years old, just 2 years into my nursing career as I embarked on a 3 month travel nursing assignment

Coming to the realization that I hated being a midwife, just 9 months (yes, ironically) after completing my Masters in Nursing, specializing as a Certified Nurse-Midwife, and deciding to walk away even though it looked like failure

Walking up to a stranger that I knew of only through Twitter and introducing myself and my business and asking for a favour ... which lead to the subsequent re-launch of my business and the birth of the Shift Change podcast

Looking back at these moments, I can clearly see how they completely changed the trajectory of my life. In the moment, however, they just felt uncomfortable, scary, and unnerving. It's that feeling of discomfort that lets you know you are pushing your comfort zone, you are expanding your limitations, you are pushing through to your next level.

Much of my career in my 20's was guided by that feeling. As soon as I started feeling too comfortable about my job, I would look for a change. Travel nursing was the perfect remedy for this, I could move to a new place and new job every 6 weeks - 3 months depending on the contract. If I loved it, I could stay longer. My skills rapidly grew during the 18 months that I spent as a travel nurse. I was able to learn best practices from so many people and observe "the best" nurses in each facility (and also, what not to do or become). Combining all the tips and tricks from each place into my own practice, I was able to further my career considerably more than had I stayed where the status quo was revered and not challenged. The phrase "because this is the way it's always been done" is detrimental to your growth, to the expansion of your comfort zone, to your ability to evolve and advance your life.

Where can you break out of your status quo and expand your comfort zone? In business, there are unlimited opportunities for personal growth and in fact, growth is required if you want to succeed. Creating a growth action plan and seeking out mentors, classes or support you need to grow those skills will put you on a path to success. Public speaking, video marketing, networking in person, these are all activities that carry a fair amount of anxiety and fear for many people. These are the activities that have the potential to change your life and business, and all that is required is 20 seconds of insane courage. Say yes to those moments, those opportunities ... your life.

While there are countless other courageous moments that have shaped my life; I'm even more keenly aware of the moments that I didn't choose courage, where I played it safe. I am left with the wonder of what may have happened had I simply chose courage instead of fear.

Brené Brown in her talk "Why Critics Aren't the Ones Who Count" she references the speech given by Theodore Roosevelt, 1910 in which he makes mention of "the man in the arena"; the person who finds the courage to fight, to dare, to try.

"It is not the critic who counts; not the man who points out how the strong man stumbles, or where the doer of deeds could have done them better. The credit belongs to the man who is actually in the arena, whose face is marred by dust and sweat and blood; who strives valiantly; who errs, who comes short again and again, because there is no effort without error and shortcoming; but who does actually strive to do the deeds; who knows great enthusiasms, the great devotions; who spends himself in a worthy cause; who at the best knows in the end the triumph of high achievement, and who at the worst, if he fails, at least fails while daring greatly, so that his place shall never be with those cold and timid souls who neither know victory nor defeat." – Theodore Roosevelt, the Man in the Arena. Delivered at the Sorbonne (Paris) on April 23rd, 1910.

Success is the result of courageous action, of putting yourself into the arena, of stepping up and speaking out when everyone else is playing small and safe. Is it uncomfortable? Absolutely. Will choosing courage always guarantee success? No. But is the chance of life-altering moments worth it? Always.

The fear of failure or self-doubt robs many of us of a life that we can only dream about. Perhaps you've been feeling a stirring in your soul lately for more; to play a bigger game in your business, grow your influence and impact more people, have more meaningful connections with people, more time with your family, more time with yourself. 'More' looks different for each person, all that matters is what you do with that stirring.

20 seconds of insane courage might look like just quieting that voice in your head that's asking "and who do you think you are?!" and actually putting an idea into action. It may look like sending an email to that dream joint venture partner who could radically change the trajectory of your business. It may look like having an honest conversation with yourself about how you have been truly showing up and where you need to spend some time working on yourself. Maybe it's having a conversation with a spouse, a friend, a business partner about your dreams and plans and the support you need from them to make it a reality. Asking for what you need can be hard but in my opinion, living with 'what-ifs' is harder.

"All that matters is whether we did what we could with the life that was given to us." — Krishna Udayasankar,

So here's what I encourage you to do…

Take a moment to look back over your life. Where are your moments of 20 seconds of insane courage? Where have you found yourself in the arena? And, perhaps the more difficult question, where have you not?

Self-doubt + reflection + growth plan + ACTION = leaning into your potential and fulfilling your dreams

Self-doubt + negative self-talk + giving up, hiding out or quitting = unfinished dreams and lives of regret

It's up to you to choose. There is HARD in making a change. In speaking up. In taking the next step in your career, in stepping up to that next level. But there is also HARD in staying stuck, playing small and hiding out. You get to choose your hard.

It's time to stop putting your dreams and desires on the shelf. Nothing changes if no one changes.

Go to http://amydeagle.com to download your FREE copy of To Do: YOU - 7½ Ways to Get Back to Yourself, a guide to giving yourself permission to become a priority in your life again! Choose you and change your life.

ABOUT AMY DEAGLE

Amy Deagle, a self-proclaimed catalyst for change who believes that self-leadership is the key to creating positive change in your life, career, and in the world.

As a masters-prepared nurse with a passion for leadership, Amy endeavours to lead a revolution of women who lead with kindness, empathy, compassion and have a desire to create more connection in the world.

She is the founder & CEO of the International Network of Nurse Leaders, host of the Shift Change podcast for nurses and author of the forthcoming book "Unshelf Yourself" for women who need to put themselves back on their priority list. A small-town girl at heart, she is a country music junkie, thinks tequila is her superpower and has been known to wear high heels in the cow-pasture.

AMY DEAGLE

CATHY MCKINNON

SET YOURSELF UP FOR SUCCESS

As a transformation coach I preach the importance of rituals for both your mind and body.

Rituals or the small things we choose to do daily have a profound effect on how successful our days are. We have the ability to dramatically change the trajectory of our days by simply tweaking things we routinely do. It is incredible to think how much we can transform the outcome of our days by taking the time to set ourselves up for success.

Now more than ever, women are feeling the pressure to do more and be more; it can be very overwhelming and depressing. Many women fall victim to the pressures of today's society and continue in careers, schedules and routines that have them feeling trapped.

I've felt this same pressure on my journey.

When we actively start to understand how to lead ourselves first, we begin to transition into the most powerful person we could be.

The reality is that we all have the same amount of time in our days and days in a week; the variable is how we CHOOSE to spend the time. Every day we make choices in how we spend our time and the results we hope that will bring. We are trading our most precious commodity, time, for a result that will hopefully net us progress/achievement.

In today's society we are juggling so many roles; entrepreneur, mother, etc. that the pull on our time is great. You must take the time to step back and assess if the choices you make daily, your habits, routines and full schedule you are grinding through each day, are still serving the path you want your life to proceed down. Understanding and creating boundaries on your time will allow you to have focus and momentum towards your goals instead of trading time for things that are not even on your radar.

"How you do one thing is how you do everything". We have seen this quote many times and yet it rings so true. If your calendar is overwhelmed, likely so is your mind, so is your household, so is your body.

Through my own transformational journey, I was shocked to learn how many people feel trapped by their lives, schedules, and jobs. They speak of how they must do this or that NOT they get to do this. They speak of the items on their calendar as if they are a chore not something that lights them up.

When you begin to establish habits that set your day and week up for success you will start to show up differently. While implementing any new habit or routine can take time the more consistently you follow this simple habit the smoother your days will go and your days will flow with ease. You will begin to operate with peace in your soul knowing that you are taking steps in the direction you have always desired.

The habits and routines you implement will allow you to operate at your best self. These are the small things you do each day to set yourself up for success. That being said, one thing we can all do is operate more intentionally. We are more often than not rushing through our days in an almost robotic mode, not being present in each moment. When we are operating in this mode we miss out on so much and create unnecessary stress and anxiety.

One success habit that has become an anchor in my routine is, looking at my calendar each evening to ensure I am prepared for the next day ahead. This allows me to ensure that I am showing up intentionally and present for what is calling my attention.

Looking at your calendar and asking the following questions will ensure you are set up for success:

Have I allowed enough time for my morning/evening routines?

Am I prepared for all the events and meetings?

Does it still fit with my schedule to attend everything as originally scheduled?

Are there items in your calendar that you should or really want to do; however, they do not fully align with your vision?

When you originally penciled in that community event you had all intention to attend however now that the day is closer you are feeling overwhelmed by all the commitments and it doesn't bring you the original joy around attending or, even worse, it means more stress having to run around town to get there on time?

Have I allowed time for self-care and fun?

Eliminate items that no longer fit where you can, of course there will always be some things that will require our attention even if they do not fit with the energy of the week. Allowing yourself time to clearly make decisions intuitively as opposed to hastily in a stressed state will give you peace in your soul knowing you took the time and thought process to work through it. Making these decisions in a clear and conscious state will allow you to increase productivity towards your vision in a way that is mindful and fulfilling.

This type of mental preparation is key and will help you to ease your anxiety for the week, help reduce those moments where you are scrambling last minute and set boundaries around your energy. We miss so much when we are rushing around robotically in "busy mode". Protecting your energy in this way will allow you to be more mindful and present to those around you, being able to take in the moments and make decisions clear headed.

Whether it is weekly, daily or monthly, I highly encourage you to take time to mentally prepare for your agenda on the calendar. Allowing yourself clarity around your days, gives you space and capacity to then deal with the inevitable changes that happen, with far less stress than dealing with it all at the last minute.

This is not about doing more as we have limited hours in the day. What this is about is filling your schedule with so many positive things, so many things that are getting you closer to the life that you envision that the negativity no longer has space in your life. It is creating a personalized path to your vision for your future, it is the greatest thing you can allow yourself.

When you take the time to make conscious decisions, it will ensure your actions are in

alignment with your goals and vision for your life. Uncluttering your schedule will allow you to create time and space to do more of what lights you up and brings you joy.

The decision around which items ultimately make your calendar must be unique, personalized, continuously re-evaluated and address all aspects of life. You must constantly ask yourself, "Does this action align with my vision?" If the answer is no, it is not something you should spend much time on. Ensuring you are taking actions that align with your purpose will allow you to achieve your goals much quicker.

The greatest way to lead yourself and therefore your legacy is to choose to live intentionally and filled with purpose starting with how you spend your days!

The sooner you start integrating success habits and ensuring you are showing up authentically for yourself and those around you the sooner the universe will bring opportunities into your energy that you could never have imagined!

Allowing that shift to happen will change where and how you show up in this world.

Your gifts and magic are so powerful that when you show up and lead yourself your impact will be felt by those around you.

To lead your legacy, you must lead yourself first protecting your energy and ensuring you are leading your days and actions with intention.

When you step into your power by creating time and space to do the things that are important and light you up it will ensure that you are living your best life. At the end of the day the one thing everyone asks for is more time; give yourself the greatest gift and give yourself back time by ensuring you are living intentionally!

Remember, you are always one decision away from a more powerful you! What are you waiting for?

Learn how to live a happy life and conquer each day with peace inside your soul with my FREE Happiness Bundle at https://www.subscribepage.com/. Start today towards that confident, energetic, joyful life you desire!

ABOUT CATHY MCKINNON

Transformation Coach, 3x International Best-Selling Author, and founder of WellnessWarriorCoaching.com.

Cathy helps women take back their lives, stepping into their power, taking them from exhausted and operating robotically to joyful and confident!

It is time for you to become the healthiest, happiest, most inspired version of yourself.

Cathy bravely shares her journey through infertility, finding her joy and reclaiming her life with her chapters in "Silent Grief, Healing and Hope", "Joy-Recipes for Abundance" and "Oh My Health there is Hope!" The books include stories that will inspire and touch hearts everywhere!

DANA PEEVER

COURAGEOUS DECISION MAKING: JUST LIKE RIDING A BIKE

I was working with a client a few years ago; he was an athlete. He had been playing in one local league at the rep level for five years and loved everything to do with the sport, his teammates, his coaches, you name it. The only thing he had started to notice was that his skill level hadn't been improving as rapidly as he'd hoped. After much deliberation, he'd narrowed the reason down to the caliber of teammates and opponents he was playing with. They were of similar abilities, so there wasn't much pushing him to improve, especially in a game situation. One other thing he'd forgotten to consider was that, as part of his spot on the rep team, his current league also required him to play during the week at the house league level. Although he played an age group up, it was still something that was frustrating and a waste of time, in his opinion.

He'd learned about another league in town that offered everything his league did, although the players were perceived to be at a higher level. They spent all of their playing time against opponents of equal or better caliber with no house league commitments. They also competed in many weekend tournaments, some internationally. It should have been a slam dunk decision for him.

But this athlete was loyal. His team was his family, having played with some of them the whole five years. His coaches were great and had spent many hours, days and years helping him become the athlete that he was. It was a community and family he belonged to. He was hesitant to walk away from that; deep inside, he felt like a traitor. And that is what was holding him back from making his decision.

When he came to me to discuss his situation, I asked him what decision he was struggling with. He told me he had to decide whether to move to this new league or not. As I started to probe more, one of the first questions I asked him was how quickly he needed to make the decision. That always plays an important part in the process.

He told me that tryouts were coming up soon. I took a step back for a minute and said, "Wait, you haven't made the new team yet?" He looked at me a little shocked and said, "No, they are just starting the first of four tryouts this weekend." At that moment, I told him his decision was going to be so much easier to make that day than he'd ever anticipated. He was a little skeptical and asked me how. I said to him, "You've gotten too far ahead of yourself, thinking you have to decide whether or not to move leagues. The only decision you have to make today is whether or not to try out."

The audible sigh of relief that escaped him at that moment is something I'll never forget. I explained to him that by going so far down that road, he had only succeeded in overwhelming himself with the weight of all of the decisions he would have to make along the way. It was an opportune time to share with him my five-step system, to ensure he would be comfortable with the path he wound up choosing.

The first step was already complete, knowing exactly the decision he had in front of him. We'd backed it up to simply deciding if he would try out or not. The next step was just as easy. What were his options? Try out or not try out. Pretty straightforward.

The third step took a little more time and it was then that I could truly see how this decision was weighing on him. We talked about all of the factors he was taking into consideration in making this decision; things like improving his skills, practice and playing time, cost, commitment, coaches, and teammates. He wound up having a list of about 20 things that came into play.

It was the next step of the process that solidified his confidence in knowing which direction to take. I had him rate the importance of each of the factors individually, right then in his life. I knew, in that moment, that a breakthrough had occurred. Through tears, he said, "I know what my decision is. I'm going to try out. We don't need to finish." He told me it all made sense, that if he was doing the best thing for him, the easiest decision he could make was to try out. Perhaps there wouldn't be another decision to make after that if he didn't even earn a spot on the new team. The relief he experienced in that moment was a feeling I asked him to reflect upon, to remember each time he was faced with a tough decision in his life. I hoped that he'd be able to come back to this moment, recall the process and proceed with courage.

I also asked him if we could finish the final two steps, mostly so that he knew what it entailed, but also to ensure there would be no questions about the end result. He agreed.

A few weeks later, I learned that he'd been offered a spot on the new team. I was curious to see if he would need to work through that decision with me. He told me he'd already accepted it, on the spot the night the coach called, so confident had he been in the work we'd done together.

This story almost brings me to tears every time I tell it. Would you be surprised to learn that this athlete, this boy feeling such allegiance to his league and willing to work honestly and deeply through this process, was only eleven years old at the time. Eleven years old. Imagine being taught how to make tough decisions courageously at that age. What a lifetime of fabulous decision making he has ahead of him. (He wound up staying with the new league for another five years, until he promptly changed his sport and has been focused on it ever since.)

Thirty years ago, I was sitting in my university class, staring bug-eyed at an intricate and downright scary, multi-page, decision-making matrix used in psychology research. As I listened to the explanation of how it worked, my math-brain was fascinated and a little in awe. I saw so much potential in the validity of its usage. It also ignited a fire in me to figure out how I could take this information and strip it back to the basics, to find a way to translate it into an everyday usable process that would help me with future decision-making in my life.

The idea percolated through various iterations over the years. I kept it to myself for half that time, testing it over and over with decisions in my own life. Once I was confident in its benefits, flexibility and consistency of helping achieve the best results ever, I started sharing the process with those I was coaching who were facing tough decisions of their own. The response was indescribable. If I had a dollar for every time I heard, "Where has this been all my life?", well, I'd still be writing a chapter for this book; because I want YOU to ask that very same question. But I'd have a much fatter bank account as well.

Here are some of the decisions I successfully and courageously made in my early and mid-adult years using my finely tuned process.

If I should go to university

What I should study

What universities to apply to

What university to attend

If I should break up with my boyfriend

What car I should buy

If I should move in with my boyfriend (new one)

What town we should live in

What apartment we should rent

What job I should take

Where to go on vacation

If we should get married

If we should buy or rent

Where we should buy

If we should move

Where we should build a house

When we should have kids

If I should embark on a new business venture

What cabin we should rent on holidays

Should I be an entrepreneur

...to name a few

After reaching such a high level of personal success, I let my secret out of the bag and started guiding others to more confident decision-making in my coaching practice. My ultimate success ritual, and the one I can't wait to share with you, is having the courage to make great decisions day in and day out. I can honestly say that I lead a charmed life thanks to the fabulous decisions I've made over the past 30 years. That's a pretty fantastic statement to be able to make, don't you think?

I'm wondering if you've ever found yourself in a situation where you were paralyzed by a decision you were faced with, or perhaps questioning the integrity of a decision you'd already made? The part I love most about what I do is creating a sense of relief for those who feel stuck in their own vortex of decision-making. I hope you've raised your hand high in the air, saying, "Pick me, pick me. I want to know the secret to making great decisions."

One thing I've learned is that people need to be in the right mindset before they can even attempt to enact their intuition in decision-making. They need to be able to open their heads and their hearts, to clear out the cobwebs, before diving into the process.

Often, I have my clients go through a free five-day challenge as a reset; a short but effective way to allow people to dig deep into where their head's currently at. By taking a step back and spending some time with your own thoughts, it gives you the space you need to move forward. If you're interested in getting your decision-making off on the right foot, I suggest you start here with a www.yearofyouchallenge.com It has inspired some pretty remarkable changes in those brave enough to face their truths.

Once you've been able to tackle that challenge, you might be interested in learning how others have successfully worked through The Decision Smith process. My #1 International Bestselling book, The Decision to Purge: The Year the Skeletons Fell out of the Closet, features stories of heroic women, all of whom have made the tough decision to take charge of their own lives. Whether it be in the face of emotional, physical or sexual abuse, toxic relationships, divorce, blended families, or other inherently difficult situations, each woman comes out the other side, a stronger, more confident version of herself.

Once you've had a chance to gain a little insight, right-set yourself and are then prepared to tackle your own decision, the final step in my success ritual is to utilize The Decision Smith app to determine the best way forward. The app walks you through the steps previously shared above:

Identify your Decision

List your Options

Define your Factors

Rate your Factors

Score your Options

Once you input all of this information into the app, the results provide you with a mathematical score and percentage pointing you in the right direction. As you use this system over and over, you'll be more confident in your own intuition, in turn increasing your decision-making success.

This book is about rituals, things you need to do over and over to become better at, to make it a habit. The same holds true about decision making. It takes practice, perseverance, honesty, and courage. But once you master the art of The Decision Smith System, it's just like riding a bike. In no time at all, you'll be doing it with no hands.

Here's to your future success in making the best decisions of your life.

ABOUT DANA PEEVER

Dana is the Creator of The Decision Smith App and The Decision Smith 5-Step System, #yearofyou challenger, #1 Best-Selling Author of The Decision to Purge: The Year the Skeletons Fell Out of the Closet, and decision expert at TheDecisionSmith.com.

On top of her zest for life, both her passion and success stem from helping people face their toughest decisions.

Having started off pursuing a psychology degree, she ultimately graduated with a Bachelor of Commerce Degree in Human Resources, Minor in Business Communications, from Ryerson University in downtown Toronto, Canada. Her long and successful career has seen her at every level of HR, but she's never strayed far from her first love of psychology. Mention social or industrial psychology and you'd better pull up a chair. And perhaps a glass of wine.

She lives with her husband and two kids on the shores of Lake Ontario west of the city. To celebrate a milestone birthday recently, she decided it was time to do something for herself after having been on call as a mom and wife for what seemed like forever. The #yearofdana was a resounding success and she has the tattoo to prove it.

MITCH MULLOOLY

IN ORDER TO HAVE, YOU FIRST MUST BE.

"Decide what you want to be, do and have, think the thoughts of it, emit the frequency, and your vision will become your life.: ~ Rhonda Byrne

To start, I want to introduce you to an especially important concept that can radically transform the quality of your life and the success of your business.

Often, we hear about, are guided by, or personally and professionally utilise the acronym SMART. This relates to goals that are Specific, Measurable, Achievable, Relevant and Timebound. I used this model myself for years to structure many of my thoughts, plans and objectives, both in my personal life and professional leadership roles, and although great for getting things done, this process never entirely gelled with me or that of realising my full potential, especially when it came to my business.

I really did feel as if I were only going through the motions and never wholly stretching myself as these goals, by the sheer nature of the acronym, were always achievable and always relevant to my current situation, and deep down inside I wanted something more.

A wee while ago I encountered a different model for setting and achieving goals. The Be-Do-Have Model. Believe me, these three little words have so much power in them, power I never expected! It has radically transformed my life and my business from the inside out.

You see, most entrepreneurs and business owners are running their businesses, and in some instances their lives, completely backwards.

Reactively.

Or how I call it: with conditions or 'playing small.'

That is the Have-Do-Be Model.

The one where you're often thinking - "Once I have the time, or once I have the money, have the resources, have the permission, have the certification… then I can do the things I need to do, and then I'll be successful, and then I'll finally be happy."

The problem with this though… when we are always waiting for our circumstances to change before we change… nothing changes.

Ask yourself - has the timing ever been right? Have I ever had enough time? Enough energy? Enough money? Enough permission?

NO.

So, what happens?

Nothing.

This is precisely why people stay stuck, often never realising their true life's potential or having the business of their dreams. A life and business that is tremendously successful on every level, one that is sustainable, highly resilient no matter what type of global crisis might get chucked at it, and well balanced with all the other aspects of the life that they truly desire to lead. It is often nothing but a fleeting dream.

The Be-Do-Have Model is one that allows us to achieve more of what we really want, and to achieve this more effectively, efficiently, and courageously.

As Stephen Covey states in his book, The 7 Habits of Highly Effective People -'You must begin with the end in mind'.

This has been one of the most influential books that I have ever read and one that I highly recommend everyone should read.

But, to 'begin with the end in mind' - what does that actually mean?

To break it down to the very basics, it means that if we do not have a clear vision of the outcome that we truly want, then technically we are sailing in open waters without any mapping or navigation guidance. No one would go out on a sailing boat without some type of GPS coordinates, mapping, or navigation guide.

Why? Because you might just find yourself lost in the middle of the vast wide ocean.

The same applies with your life, with your business, with your success, in whatever facet you want that in, whether it be your health, wealth, love, and happiness. You must begin with the end in mind and hold that outcome in your vision. We must define success for ourselves.

Whenever I do something, I have an intent behind it. There is an intent that I want this particular desired outcome however I do not let that intent overwhelm the things that I am doing. If I am trying to make money, or I am trying to sell a certain number of coaching spots, or pre-launch a coaching programme, I'm not hyper-focused on 'I need to sell this many to be successful'. But instead, I have the intent that the goal is to sell this many so I will work at that by doing the actions that will lead to the success and the desired outcome I am seeking.

So, what is your desired outcome?

I see a lot of people out there just mindlessly drifting in the wind, never having any clear vision, no true clarity around what they actually want. They are consuming a vast array of information from so many different sources and advice from all manner of other people, often letting comparison-mode set in. Or taking instruction from multiple different mentors and coaches, and not purposely focusing on one set vision. They have no one set outcome to what they genuinely want, and they are literally just traveling in the slipstream. You will find it exceedingly difficult to be successful with that type of approach. You must 'begin with the end in mind.'

So, we must start with a HAVE. A Result.

Ritual #1 – Gain clarity

What are you wanting to achieve? Identify a result that would have you knowing for a fact that you have made real progress in your life and in your business.

Take a moment to write that down now.

Grab your journal, or a piece of paper, and physically write it down.

Did you do that?

Next, let us take a moment to check in on this result.

Is it monetary?

If it is not, that is going to have to change. In life you need money to pay expenses and in business its growth is about revenue and profit. If you are not focusing on goals that grow your profit or sales, how do you expect your business to grow, how do you expect to even stay in business?

You may not think money is that important, but your business sure needs it, and just think how much more impact you will be able to create when you are making more money. So, with that said, hopefully your goal is revenue based, if not, change it now! This also means that your result is measurable, and it must also have a specific due date.

Next, take a moment and write it out in the present tense. For example: it is now the 31st December, year 20_ _ and I have generated $25,000 in sales.

Make sure you take the time to write this out, as the act of actually doing this exercise is where the transformation begins.

Now, if we take a look back at our Be-Do-Have Model, then you know that a result such as generating $25k by December 31 isn't possible without any action.

Right?

Without the actual doing!

Ritual #2 – Do the right things, the right way

Next, you are going to need to identify what you are going to do to get you there. However, it is not just about doing, it is about doing the right things, the right way. And that is determined by your being.

Being is who you choose yourself to be in any given moment, at any given time. It is the sum total of your thoughts, of your beliefs, your emotions, your internal state.

You already have the ability to know when you are being confident, you know when you are being loving. You also know when you are being distracted, becoming unmotivated, and are allowing fear or limiting beliefs to cloud your view.

But these states are a choice, because all of life is a choice, and in this present moment you can choose who you are.

So how will you show up for the world, for your audience, your customers, for you?

This is where you do not have to choose who you may have been in the past.

Often, when people say that they are a failure, or they are useless at creating content, or are a slow learner, they are simply taking the experiences of their past, and choosing in this present moment who they are going to be in their future, which is more of who they have already been... in the past.

But you can become someone with limitless potential.

The only reason we set a goal, is not about the realization of that goal, it is about who you get to discover yourself to be, in the pursuit of that goal.

So, to break it down even further, the Be-Do-Have Model performs like this, when you identify what you want to have, you must then identify who you need to be, in order to make that goal a reality.

Ritual #3 – Determine who you need to be and be them now

So, who do you need to be in order to accomplish this goal?

Or another way to approach this is if you had already accomplished this goal, who would you be? How would it feel? What would you think? What would you believe?

Then, every day, you choose to be that version of you, now.

It is that person who will do the right things the right way, to get you the results you have always wanted.

That is where every moment becomes a choice. Are you going to be the old version of you, the one that got you here to this moment, or are you going to choose the new version of you, who knows that your success is inevitable?

BE – think about the type of person you want to be, how you want to be treated like, how you want to treat others and how you approach things like your challenges, relationships, finances, health and personal development. Think about the type of attitude, values, character and beliefs you need to have to be that person.

Be the person who has the clarity and the confidence, the vision and the belief, the structure and the consistency, the strategy and the courage to truly make your life and your business successful beyond your wildest dreams.

This is the work that makes the difference.

And even if you are struggling with this... that's okay. The majority do at first. But I'm here to help you!

When you are clear about who you want to be, you will have little to no issues in finding out what you need to do.

DO – now that you have established the type of person you want to be, make a list of things and actions that you must take to fulfil the role of the person you are working on becoming. You can even take it further by altering the way you dress, talk and interact with others. Do the necessary work, in order to have the necessary outcome.

HAVE – once you are being the person you want to be, you will start acting and making decisions that will bring or attract what you want to have. Having is the result of you being and doing.

BE – DO – HAVE

Choose to change your mindset and strategy from the Have-Do-Be Model to the Be-Do-Have Model and truly experience the power of these three little words!

Can't quite see yet how this all fits together? Here is my example:

Have-Do-Be Model

When I have the necessary skills, I will start a coaching business and help my clients with successful goal setting.

Be-Do-Have Model

I am a Coach, therefore I am going to upskill and develop myself, so I can help my clients achieve successful goal setting.

BE the person, that can DO what it takes to reach the HAVE - the goal.

Changing your being will affect what you do, which in turn will be followed by the results you desire. We are human 'beings' after all!

What is immensely powerful about this is that you do not have to start creating goals by making them super specific from the very beginning, as that can be truly daunting. Start by simply letting your imagination flow and just write down the thoughts that I am fairly sure you have in your head already. You can write more than one thing in each of those parts and then try to explore which ones are at the core, which ones resonate deeply with you.

But what if you want to be more than just one thing?

So, you wrote down several things that you want to be, do and have, and that's totally okay, I do! You generally have more than one role and more than one need in your life. You may be a parent, a leader, a friend, and a cook. The point of this exercise however is to look at them now and see what is really hidden below all of them. This will help you decide which ones will be your most visual signposts, and which ones will be the guidelines for your decisions in the next few months or years.

Thanks to really looking deeper into the things you wrote down, you can see whether your desires, needs and dreams align or whether some of them may be contradictory. Contradictory ones can for example include balancing work and family commitments, where you want to travel the world with work but also want to spend a lot of time with family, making memories.

Dig deep and discover who you truly desire to BE. Implement the actions and DO what is required to HAVE this result, the life that you truly can not get enough of.

And that is my intention for you!

"Until you make peace with who you are, you'll never be content with what you have." ~ Doris Mortman

ABOUT MITCH MULLOOLY

Mitch Mullooly is a Health and Wellness Strategist specialising in the wellbeing of emergency first responders. Mitch has spent more than two decades in the pre-hospital medical environment and has a long-held passion for healthy living and wellbeing within the international emergency services community.

Mitch is the Chair of the Australasian College of Paramedicine, Aotearoa New Zealand; member of Te Kaunihera Manapou, New Zealand Paramedic Council; Advisory Committee member for Te Kiwi Māia - The Courageous Kiwi; and proud recipient of the Council of Ambulance Authorities (Australasia) - Women in Ambulance Honour, 2020. Mitch is also a published author, speaker and feature columnist for several industry related magazines, blogs, webinars, and podcasts.

Mitch is wahine toa of Ngāi Tahu descent, the principal Māori iwi (tribe) of the South Island of Aotearoa New Zealand. She lives in a stunningly beautiful region on the East Coast of the North Island with her husband, also an emergency first responder, and their young son. As a family they own and run a commercial citrus orchard and love making memories by enjoying the beautiful long white sandy beaches and stunning native bush surrounding their home.

To find out how Mitch can help you reverse the negative effects of physical and psychological fatigue to make you fit for duty and ultimately fit for life, head to http://www.eattrainbelieve.com to claim your free downloadable Healthy Habits Guide and wellbeing resources.

SUSAN ELFORD

ACTIVATE YOUR BUSINESS POTENTIAL WITH THE POWER OF PR

How do you do it? My clients, friends and colleagues have asked me this repeatedly over the years. How do you keep your business going?

I often give them a smile – sometimes an eye roll – and then I say, "It's a lot of work."

My response is often accompanied with a sigh.

Yes, a sigh.

Because it's not easy.

There's no magic pill you can swallow that will have you wake up tomorrow with all your dreams fulfilled. There must be a reason behind why you keep showing up every day.

What are you doing it all for?

What keeps you going, each and every day?

It wasn't until recently, when I found myself answering questions about my success as a solo-entrepreneur that I realized I actually did have repeatable "secrets" to my success that were keeping me going through the 18 years I've been in business.

These are the secrets that will be revealed to you here.

You will be happy to know that two of them are not knowledge-based. They're not things you have to learn in school or study. One is the why behind what you do – why you show up every day; another is a way of being – the way you show up every day; and then of course, there's the how you do it that makes it all happen, a way of doing.

We'll cover all three here.

But first, why should you listen to me? What the heck do I know about any of this?

If we take a flashback to the corporate executive I was before launching my first business in 2003, you'll see the picture of a highly educated, focused, and committed corporate communications executive who loved her job. I was working in a large, international energy company and I was on the way UP. At the age of 32 I had already served at the highest levels of government and organizations and I enjoyed being a part of a successful company that had a significant impact on the world's economic engine.

My work felt important. Like I was making a contribution that mattered and that I was making a meaningful impact and was relied upon for my expertise and talents.

And then my husband and I decided to have a family. Couples have been having children since the beginning of time, yet for some reason, this simple next step in the journey of life practically derailed me. Giving birth to a beautiful bundle of energy who was my daughter got my head and my heart all confused as I no longer had the same passion for my work that kept me away from her for most of her waking hours. My husband was also enjoying a successful career and while we could afford childcare and could make choices to raise our daughter through other people, it was not the choice I wanted to make. I found myself quickly realizing that I wanted to claim more control of my time so I could fit my work into my life vs. my life into my work and most of all, spend more time with my baby girl.

And that for me, meant resigning my used-to-be dream job and starting in the world as an independent communications consultant.

I launched Elford Communications and quickly found myself picking up contracts and juggling Mom-hood fairly well, I thought. I had control of my time and could pick and choose my clients. What's more, I didn't advertise. I didn't have a website. I didn't launch expensive marketing campaigns. I built my entire business based on referrals and using good old-fashioned public relations tools that I had been implementing in my client and employer's organizations throughout my career.

This journey of providing consulting services as a company of one had many ups and downs for sure. Many "up's," and then a "down" -- or more of a question mark, 10 years in, led me to hire my first coach to help me figure out what I most wanted next for my career and business. That journey of re-discovering what I wanted for me led me to training as a personal leadership and business coach to support other women going through their journey's of figuring out the best equation for their life and work.

And so I started another business in 2015 – Susan Elford Coaching & Consulting - to serve ambitious, big-hearted women to uncover and then build the life, career and or business of their dreams.

And again, I used the same repeatable ways of building a business and attracting repeatable and consistent work that I had in my communications consulting practice.

And that's what I'm going to offer you here – those three key things that have been the success rituals I had intuitively adapted, time and time again, in the now 18 years I have been a solo-entrepreneur.

1) Know your WHY

If you have been around this world of building your business and uncovering your "what's next?" for a while, then the idea of knowing your "why," uncovering your life's purpose and tapping into that inner drive that has you get out of bed each more with enthusiasm may not be new to you.

For those of you who have this deep inner knowing, the knowledge of what you have been put on this earth to do, and the desire to make a difference for yourself and others, then you can skip to point #2. But for those of you who aren't sure what this is – you may be uncertain what 's calling you and you have a desire to find out – then this is your best first step.

Knowing my why has made all the difference. It keeps me going every day, it's my anchor that I hold onto when the going gets tough, and it's the reason why I am excited to go to work everyday. It's also THE key thing that has ensured my business has been profitable and consistent, year after year.

When you know your why, and you keep sight of that why every day, you will more often choose "showing up" rather than "giving up."

My Success Ritual #1: Understand your why, honour your why and keep it front and centre so that it keeps you motivated each and every day.

2) Be Consistent

This is part of your way of being. Regardless of who you are, what you do or why you do it, if you do what you do consistently you will be successful. F-O-C-U-S: Follow One Course Until Successful the old adage says, and this simple tool cannot be underestimated.

If you decide to write a newsletter to keep your community engaged and interested, for example – keep doing it. If you decide to offer a kind of service or product – commit to offering that service or product reliably, time after time, so that you can confidently be referred to by your friends, family and colleagues who know you will do what you say you will do.

Keep showing up, keep doing the thing, and be THAT person who is relied upon to deliver that service, offer that product, and be, do and deliver that thing that you say you are going to do. This will activate your referral network (covered more in point #3) and is key behind ensuring your referral network grows, and consequently your business grows.

This isn't rocket science – this is a way of being that is committed to showing up – consistently. And while this concept isn't complicated, it's not always easy. What will keep you showing up and becoming relied upon to deliver those consistent results or product is your WHY – see point #1. IF you know and honour your why, this will help you honour point #2 – consistently showing up.

My Success Ritual #2: Choose your path and stick to it. Be consistent. Keep showing up. Become that business owner who can consistently be relied upon to deliver their service or product in the way they say they will.

3) Be Your Own PR Person

OK, this is a big one and I'll introduce the basic concepts here. This is your way of doing. The how you do what you do, and a big reason for my repeatable, continued success over the years are the many tools of public relations that I developed a habit of implementing in my business.

At the core of an effective Public Relations Strategy for your business are what I like to call the 5 R's. These are:

i. Research

ii. Relationships

iii. Responsibility

iv. Reputation

v. Results

i. Research

The key tenant of any public relations strategy is knowing who you're talking to and why. This is work you will have done in building your business plan. Once you know who you're talking to and who you're building relationships with, you can uncover what they need support with, what they would most want from you, where they get their information, where the best place is to reach them, and so on. Also knowing what has worked before, what they would pay you (almost) anything for, and knowing their motivators are all key things that will support you as you build your PR plan. In short, knowing your audience, doing research about that audience, and researching the best ways to build relationships with them is the first step in building your Public Relations Strategy for your business.

ii. Relationships

Honestly, at the root of any public relations strategy or program, are relationships. People buy from people, especially if you're a small business. So building your business in the context of building effective public relationships will ensure you are connecting with your customers or clients, meeting them where they are, and understanding how you can best serve them. Who do you most want to build relationships with in your business, and why? Where are your ideal customers spending their time? Get out there in real life and meet them, get to know them – and connect with them in online social spaces. All of these will build a two-way connection that will build your understanding of them, and them of you.

iii. Responsibility

This goes back to my Success Ritual #2 – of being consistent in your behaviour. Can your customers or clients trust you? Are you going to do what you say you are going to do? Are the promises behind your service or product reliable? Good Public Relations is highly ethical. Never say you are doing something you're not. Be a responsible and ethical business owner and your clients will trust you.

Another way to look at this tenant of Public Relations is what does it mean to you to be a responsible business owner? Are you a part of a global green future? Do your societal and political views align with what you believe in and stand for as a company? Can you stand up for what you believe in and have actions to put behind the words of your promotional strategy? Ensuring the actual doing of your company lines up with what you say you're going to do is critical to your business success.

iv. Reputation

Now you've done your research, you are building effective two-way relationships and you are acting responsibly, what do you think will happen with your business reputation? It will be golden. Building your business, organization or personal reputation is the key driver behind a successful public relations strategy. What do you want to be known for in your business? What do you stand for? What are the mission, vision and values of your organization? Knowing them and living up to them are the essence behind your organization's reputation.

v. Results

And what are we doing all this for? Results, that's what for. You are putting all this effort into showing up consistently and building a public relations strategy for your business so that you can build a successful business. Deciding what you want your results to be before building a plan to get there has been at the root of many company successes – there are also many business owners who fly by the seat of their pants and somehow get there too. For myself, I like to plan. I like to start with the end in mind and build my plan to get me there. This shows up in consistent, repeatable results in my business, year over year.

My Success Ritual #3: Build a Public Relations Strategy for your business using the 5 R's of Public Relations: Research, Relationships, Responsibility, Reputation, and Results. Consistent and strategic implementation of these practices will ensure you can achieve repeatable success in your business and activate a 6th R – Referrals!

Here we touched on why you should consider building a public relations strategy for your business. It's one of my top 3 success rituals that lead to a referrals and relationship-based business, and ensures you continue to achieve results.

You will have the opportunity to dive deeper into these topics through a free download from my website, Your PR Launchpad which includes a complimentary review and PR strategy session with me.

I'm looking forward to seeing what you have in store for that dream business of yours. Stop being the world's best kept secret and use the Power of PR to Activate your Business Potential.

Get your copy of the PR Launchpad at https://susanelford.com/pr-launchpad/

ABOUT SUSAN ELFORD

Susan Elford, APR, CPCC, PCC is a Leadership Coach, Business Builder and Community Leader who is at her best when bringing women together in community to build meaningful and purposeful careers and businesses.

Her 28-year career as a PR Strategist has seen Susan serving at the highest levels of corporations, governments and not-for-profit organizations, with 18 of those years as the President of Elford Communications, her PR Consultancy.

As a certified Leadership Coach, Susan works 1:1 and in groups of professional women and business builders as they navigate the growth of their successful careers and businesses, on their own terms. Susan's passion for supporting ambitious women on their business and career journey's, plays out in her volunteer work as well. Susan is the Founder and President of Lean in Calgary, Canada's latest addition to the global network of Lean in Leaders.

A huge part of Susan's "why" is wrapped up in her family life as wife to Rod and mother to Amanda and Kate, their two teenage daughters. Building lasting memories with them while building a successful business is her proudest success.

You can find out more about Susan's private, group, and online offerings for growing business owners at www.susanelford.com

SUE HENRY

BE EVERYWHERE YOUR PROSPECTS ARE

Ah, social media.

It offers all the excitement and hope for a profitable business and personal fulfillment... yet it also carries the stress and frustration of feeling like a time-trap with nothing to really show for it.

Ever feel that way?

See, it's easy for us to fall into the trap of thinking we need to constantly create new content and post constantly for our "stuff" to be put in front of our ideal prospects. And that creates a lot of stress and anxiety...

But nothing can be further from the truth!

It's not enough for someone to see our post, check out our social media profile, or visit our website once. Statistics and the gurus tell us that our prospects need to see us multiple times (7-12 times) before they will take action... you can't grow a sustainable and lucrative business as a "one-stop wonder".

So, it's UP TO US to make sure we are out there in a way that makes us "stalk-worthy" and our ideal prospects feel like they are seeing us EVERYWHERE!

Before you get all weirded out about being "stalk-worthy", let me explain. I'm not talking about some creepy stalker with even creepier intentions…

I'm talking about your content and presence being so exciting and relevant to what they are looking for that your ideal prospects keep coming back to see what you are up to and what you are offering!

Make sense?

Most people scroll through their feeds looking for something that catches their attention as a distraction from their otherwise boring lives… (I know I do – especially when I'm putting off doing something I don't want to! I try to pretend that I'm "working" when I'm really not…)

You could post pictures and videos of puppies, kittens, etc., and stop the scroll.

But since our ideal prospects are also looking for what we offer (products or services), we need to find a way to blend "cute" with "compelling".

The goal is for our ideal prospects to see us all over social media and make us look like we are a much "bigger" personality than we may actually be…

And let's keep in mind that we are pretty dang busy people. Who has time to post every couple of hours?

Or keep coming up with new content?

Or spend money on targeting ads that may or may not drive in new paying clients or customers to us and what we offer?

Or try and stay on top of FB's latest algorithm changes?

There's an easier way, my friend!

Imagine…

What if you had an easy-to-implement system to take charge of your online presence, increase engagement, and improve your conversions of prospects into actual clients?

Hmm… Sound good? It's simple, really.

It's all about repurposing the content we create (or have created in the past) and in a strategic, intentional, and deliberate method.

Trust me, once you get the hang of the daily success ritual, you will thank your lucky stars that you read and implemented this!

It's like being handed the "easy" button for social media marketing!

Before I get into the nitty-gritty of the daily activity, I'd like to share a couple of tips you may find helpful:

You can create all of your posts on Sunday. This works great for those will full-time positions – you get it done in one swoop and even if your job (or life) gets super crazy during the week, you are prepared!

Use a service like Evernote (free) to upload your personal profile posts and images. I upload on my computer because it's easier for me to work on it but everything I create is also in the smartphone app. It only takes a couple of minutes to pull up the post and image you created and then copy and paste into your profile.

You can pre-schedule posts on your business page within FB. No need to use a 3rd party service. (And FB doesn't like these services, either. They want you actively engaging and will ding you if you try to shortcut the posting process through a 3rd party app.

You can use the same post on your biz page and personal profile as long as you make a couple of tweaks: change the wording in the post just a little or add an emoji; make a subtle change to your picture or image. I suggest using Canva – even if you just change the color of your text or background, FB views it as "new" content and will deliver it without hurting your algorithm. Plus, Canva has some great photos for FREE and if you choose to buy one, they are only $1. A steal!

You'll also make a change to your post/image if you are posting on Instagram.

Your blog post can be published as an article on LinkedIn. Be sure to include appropriate hashtags.

Sunday: Choose your theme for the week.

Everything you create should be about this theme with different spins… For this example our topic will be "having a home business".

Example: Some of my friends talk about "sour stomach Sunday's" and "headache Monday's" because they don't like their jobs but they feel trapped. I used to feel the same way… but I finally gave myself permission to explore building my own business in the little nooks and crannies of my busy days. And I'm so glad I did! Now I look forward to Sunday's because it's when I take time to be present with my family, friends, and do the things I enjoy without the dark cloud above my head of having to head back to a toxic work environment." Then I'd post an image of me doing something I enjoy… my garden, my cows, my family, etc.

Monday Motivation: Write a blog post.

Example: 3 Things I Wish I'd Known About Starting My Home Business That Would Have Helped Me Get Clients (or customers) Sooner! Create and post 2 social media posts with different images and a link to your blog post. Be sure to keep it upbeat, inspiring, and motivating! Paint a picture of what results and lifestyle your ideal prospects want – not on what they need to do to get the results. Create curiosity.

Tuesday Transformation/Testimonial.

Do a FB Live based on your blog post and include either how it's transformed you or a testimonial about someone else who is either working with you or has experienced what your target market feels and how they've had success.

Tap into their big pain… make them feel the pain so their desire to remove the pain and get what they want is intensified. You can use your facial expressions, tone of voice, and emotion to convey this in your Live. Try to keep your Live to under 10 minutes. (At least that's what is working best now. In the future? Who knows!)

Be sure to include the blog post link in the top comment in the Live. (Hint: You can use SteamYard, a free service, that will let you go Live on multiple platforms at the same time. i.e. your FB profile, FB biz page, YouTube, LinkedIn)

Wednesday: Wealth/Travel/Lifestyle.

Create and post 2 different social media posts about your topic and how it relates to one of the 3 interests.

Example: Climbing to the top of Wallace Monument (Braveheart movie was based on his life) in Scotland was definitely worth those 246 narrow little triangle-shaped steps going up a turret! My heart was touched as I learned more about the Scots and their fight to be separate from England. I'm so grateful my business gives me the flexibility to travel and still generate income from anywhere… (I'd include an image of me at the top of Wallace Monument)

Thursday Throwback.

Create/post 2 social media posts about how things used to be… either in your life, before Women's Lib, or some fun stories about you growing up and your experiences. Pictures of you as a kid or other relevant throwbacks (based on your subject) are usually high-interest and stop the scroll.

If you send emails, I'd also send out an email this day of the blog post you wrote on Monday. My highest email open rates are on Thursday and Sunday. Find when your highest open rate is and schedule your email for that day. Most autoresponders will allow you to schedule your email being sent out.

Friday Freedom: Get Personal (i.e. Cooking, Crafts, Family Activities, Hobbies).

Let people know what you've got planned for the weekend. All work and no play won't attract the people you want! LOL This can be random and you don't have to tie to some statement about having a home biz.

Example: "My 5-year old granddaughter came over and we made Christmas cookies together! Her job was to push the cookie cutter into the dough. Then, once the cookies were baked and cooled, she frosted and decorated them. When I got out all the different decorations she could add to her cookies, her eyes lit up like lights on a Christmas tree! She did a great job!". Then I'd include the photo I took of her decorating the cookies and a photo of her holding the plate with the "finished" product.

Saturday Weekend Warriors/DIY/ParentOnTheRun:

Create and post at least 1 post. For many people, weekends are insane. They are running kids here and there, catching up on errands, housework, shopping, meal prep, etc. What tips, advice, or suggestions can you share that would be helpful? What funny stories do you have about when things didn't go as you'd planned? You DO want to tie this to having a home business a little.

Example: Saturday... with 3 kids all in different activities, life is crazy. That's why I have the bumper sticker "If a mom's place is in the home, why am I always in the SUV?" haha! But seriously, I'm glad my kids want to be active and not just sit around at home staring at a screen or figuring out how to bug each other. While waiting for them to get done with practice or pack up after an activity, I get to relax or work – my choice. Sometimes I listen to music. Sometimes I play games on my smartphone. And sometimes I use the time to follow up with people I didn't get to follow up with earlier in the week. But... the good news is I GET TO CHOOSE. And that's one of the things I love about having my own biz." Then I'd include a photo of a kids activity, a screenshot of my phone playing music, me sitting in my car jamming to some music, etc.

Tip: Don't worry about what time you post — post when it's convenient for you. Let FB do the hard work of showing it to the right people at the right time for you.

Consistency is key!

And consistency is what will make your ideal prospects think you are everywhere because if they click on something of yours once, FB will do the retargeting for you!

Cool, right?

It used to take me a couple of hours on a Sunday to put this all together. But, once I got used to it, it now takes less than an hour to have it planned out for an entire week.

I save my posts and images in Evernote (free) so I have everything at my fingertips when I need it… no matter where I am!

Becoming stalk-worthy is a noble goal… these daily rituals will help you achieve this status and have your prospects going back over and over to see what you're up to next and how they can get more of "YOU"…

And isn't that the whole point of social media marketing?

If you'd like to become an influencer in YOUR niche, grab my free guide, "The Ultimate Checklist To Becoming An Influencer In Your Niche!" at https://suehenrytalks.com/checklist-to-influencer

ABOUT SUE HENRY

Sue Henry teaches women how to become influencers in their niche through her monthly FREE 5-day challenge and her coaching programs! Sue is an int'l speaker and has had more than 5,500 people from 18 countries attend one of her butts-in-seats training. She's shared the stage with Jack Canfield, Brian Tracy, Bob Burg, Ivan Misner, Keith Ferrazzi, Stephan M.R. Covey, Lisa Nichols, Janet Attwood, Ann Sieg, and more! She's also a coveted guest on podcasts.

Her coaching programs give women a step-by-step process to become an influencer in their niche. Influencers attract their ideal prospects instead of hunting for them! Every program starts with zapping and DELETING FOREVER the negative thoughts, beliefs, and lies we all have in our subconscious and unconscious. Sue's clients find that once these are eliminated, it's easier than ever to see results and achieve their goals!

Sue and her husband are organic, grass-only dairy farmers in SE Minnesota. They have 6 grown kids and 6 ADORABLE grandchildren. She loves to read regency romances, cook, road trips, and attend marketing conferences and events!

SUE HENRY

SHIVANI BHAGI

HONOUR YOUR PATH

Success. First let's talk about this word. What success means to me may be different for you, and that's ok. That's actually the point.

Blindly following a version of success that does not deeply resonate with you is the fastest way to push success further away.

In this chapter I share my story of success where;

a single "thought" triggered a domino effect in my life,

the unexpected path that opened up before me,

the quantum leaps, and

the transition to a career and life that truly aligns with who I am. (my version of success)

1. Going Against My Own Grain

It all began five years into my corporate career. I started as a grad in the IT industry working for a multinational organization. I plodded along year after year with no real direction, plan or impact.

Sure, I'd done some good pieces of work that got me some recognition, but personally I didn't experience the momentum and growth I had hoped for.

I was uninspired, it had all gotten pretty boring and then one single thought changed everything.

"Why am I going against my own grain?" Why am I doing work that I don't enjoy? Why am I tolerating things in my career just to keep my job?

I recall the exact moment; I was driving home on the A3 to Southfields, South London (near Wimbledon if you don't know London) where I lived at the time. I made a mental list in my head.

My list went something like this:

- I do lots of technical and computer code work which I don't enjoy

- I'm not using my best talents – business, creativity and people

- I'm surrounded by people who are very happy with the status quo and a slower pace

I decided there and then that I was no longer available for these things and I was not going to tolerate doing work that didn't give me joy or fulfillment. Given we spend an average of 8 hours a day at work,

"I can't waste my life away like this!" Is what went through my head.

I started to exercise my boundaries and began to say NO to the roles I no longer had interest in and instead, expressed my desire for the type of work I DID want to do.

Slowly but surely my experience started to improve and so did my level of happiness and fulfillment.

I landed a role in the consultancy arm of the firm and started doing work that excited me. The role brought out a lot of my best qualities and I even worked long days without batting an eyelid.

Every night my head hit my pillow, I felt satisfied and valued and I was ready for the next day. This was a feeling I'd NEVER had before.

I was young, hungry and longing to thrive both personally and professionally. I never considered myself particularly ambitious as some of my peers were, I just knew I had potential that was massively untapped and that was a feeling I could not live with.

This role led to a promotion, pay rise, friendships and most importantly, an experience that lit me up! Working with some super talented professionals was the icing on the cake.

I knew there and then that I couldn't go back. I knew exactly what type of people I wanted to surround myself with (talented, creative, driven people), and what type of client accounts I wanted to work on (dynamic environments where I could learn and grow).

Sadly, this experience wasn't long lived. My role came to end and after another 6 months or so on a new project, the company decided to close the business unit I belonged to and offered hundreds of us voluntary redundancies.

No one saw it coming!

I'd been with the firm for seven years! What now?

2. Deal or No Deal?

The official letters were sent to our home addresses. The company had given us the option to redeploy ourselves to a different business unit within the organization or take the redundancy package.

At that time I had just purchased my first property in London. I had mortgage payments to take care of and the timing was not ideal.

Fortunately for me, my ex manager from the consulting arm called me up as soon as he'd heard the news internally and offered me a place on his team.

Whilst truly grateful to him, I knew that the voluntary redundancy option was an opportunity being handed to me on a silver platter; I'm getting paid to leave and I'd have the chance to find a new job that would tick all the boxes that I now knew needed ticking!

A total of seven years at this company and only one year was great. I knew deep down that the bigger regret would have been not taking the package and staying stuck in a situation I knew too well. My comfort zone was actually not comfortable anymore. That was the truth. I needed to get out of it.

To many people's surprise I opted for redundancy even though I didn't have a job lined up!

That's how much I trusted and honoured my feelings. I knew I couldn't stay. It was time. Time to take a risk, which if it was to pay off, would give me the growth and excitement I was craving in my career.

So began the process of applying for new jobs with my new checklist in hand. I started attending interviews.

Exit interview day came around. The day I needed to show up at the head office in Surrey, hand in my laptop and other company equipment, have a chat with HR and close this chapter.

As if by divine timing, that SAME morning I received my offer letter through the post from a Management Consulting firm. They were offering me a 30% salary hike!

That day I truly learnt the power of setting intentions that honour our deepest desires and then keeping faith! That day changed everything for me. That day I knew I had co-created this experience with the universe.

3. Quantum Leaps

The next few years flew by. I was learning, I was growing, I was impactful, I was working with some of the best talent globally. These years absolutely shaped me further to be the person I am today.

Dormant qualities in me were sparked and elevated like never before, I was taking quantum leaps in every aspect, personally and professionally.

It was during these years where I discovered my new core value of authenticity. No longer did I want to show up as a version of me that was trying to fit in with the work culture. I wanted to be unapologetically me!

It took time and a LOT happened before I started taking steps towards the new AUTHENTIC ME.

It took a bad experience with a peer who was desperate for his promotion, it took an overwhelming amount of stress mentally which manifested physically in the form of rosacea, a condition which had developed on my face.

There was no hiding from that one, I was reminded every day when I looked in the mirror!

I actually smile with astonishment thinking back to how stressed I was (without realising it at the time) and just how much I had been pushing myself. I was so consumed I didn't even bother to wear makeup to cover up the redness on my face!

I got everything I wanted in a job, the excitement, the challenge, the growth, the dynamic and fast environment, but at what cost? The cost of my health and what was actually quite a lonely existence travelling constantly and living out of a suitcase in hotel rooms. Not so glamorous as it may seem.

It was time to take stock and reassess. I further refined my life and career vision and incorporated my evolved core values which I realised were; Freedom, Growth and Authenticity.

Things were becoming clearer with every chapter in my life because I kept asking myself the right questions; what am I tolerating? What are the consequences? What do I want instead? Which values am I compromising? What needs to change and what should my next move be?

It was clear as day. It was time to engineer an exit and move to an environment where I could grow and thrive without sacrificing my health or lifestyle needs.

It turns out I didn't need to engineer anything. The Universe did that for me.

The firm dropped one of its major accounts and gave us the option to transition over to another firm who had taken over the account.

This meant I would be back based in London with minimal travel. RESULT.

Thank you universe for listening!

But why was the universe working its magic at the perfect time?

It dawned on me.

I had committed to the decision FIRST, just like before when I decided to take the redundancy.

I honoured my decision and committed to my path FIRST without having all the answers and despite the 'risks'. It was THEN that the universe delivered.

Let that sink in. I know I had to.

4. I'm "successful", but why this void?

Fast forward three years. I'm in the new firm. I had a great job, I was one of the best in our team, I was now the owner of two properties in London, had an active social life, a new car and a great salary BUT there was a void and I couldn't put my finger on it.

As far as I knew I was living a full life. I played tennis on the weekends, and I travelled abroad at any given opportunity.

Outside of work I was studying for a coaching certification and had even taken on some coaching clients at the weekends, purely through word of mouth at my tennis club.

In addition I was organising talks at the weekends in central London with well known professionals in the personal development space. Something I enjoyed and got a lot of value from.

Why then did I still feel as if something was missing?

My day job had started to feel too routine and repetitive and somehow I knew my potential was still not fully unlocked. I was being called to a new reality and up leveling. I could feel it.

The biggest giveaway was that I started to resist my day job and looked forward to my weekend work instead.

Around the same time I kept having the desire to work and live abroad in a hot country. I loved being in a sunny climate. I felt different. It made me happy. Every time I heard someone in my circle had moved abroad I'd feel envious. That was another sign.

I put the intention out to the universe. This time I had no idea 'how' I would make this happen. I just knew I was being called to it and WOW, did the universe deliver!

5. The Calling, Manifestations and Spiritual Growth

This section VERY briefly covers the past 10 years of my life. I could actually write a book on this alone but let's cover a few highlights of the spiritual journey that I've been on (and continue to be on).

It took one holiday to India where I met someone in Goa who would not only become my business partner but one day my husband (we married in 2018).

When I met Kashif, we made plans to start a restaurant business in Goa. It was new, exciting and ticked many boxes for me. I had no experience in the restaurant industry but I had a background in business and consulting. I was eager to learn and Kashif had on the ground business experience in India.

I handed in my notice and quit the corporate life after 15 years, despite MANY telling me how damaging this could be for my career. I honoured my path and didn't let fear stop me. In fact I was so in resonance with my calling that there really wasn't much fear. Mostly excitement.

I emptied my apartment, put everything in storage, gave my car to my sister to look after, and off I went.

To this day I will never forget the indescribable feeling of looking back at the corporate headquarters of the firm I was working for, knowing that from that day onwards I was not answerable to anyone and was free to shape my own work and life experience. Free to shape my destiny!

It was one of the most freeing moments of my life.

Not only did the universe help me co-create a new life in a beautiful sunny country, I also got to meet my future husband.

Double whammy this time. Thank you Universe!

Friends back home were inspired.

"Wow! You're living the dream!" they said. The dream many people have of running an establishment by a beach.

Here's the kicker. A couple of years in I realised that this wasn't it for me, either!

My heart knew this wasn't what was going to keep me growing, excited or valuable personally or professionally. Although I cherished the experience despite the many ups and downs we faced, I knew my time here was done.

6. Flow & Success

The decision I made next created a lot of flow and ease in my life. I decided to go all in and commit fully to my coaching, mentoring and training career.

Eight years on and I haven't looked back. This business aligns so well with my values and lifestyle desires.

At the time of writing this chapter I've delivered hundreds of leadership level workshops for multinational orgs, ran career retreats for women and worked with countless clients privately as their coach and mentor.

ALL of my previous experience in corporate and business has led me to this point in my career and life. Nothing has been a waste and opportunities have literally come to me. Life has been in flow for me these past eight years.

It's my mission and passion to help as many professionals as I can to forge their purpose-driven paths, do their best work and live inspired lives!

To conclude this chapter, I want to highlight the key learnings from my journey so that it may help others who are called to powerfully step into their new level/reality.

Keep raising your awareness and keep checking in with yourself regularly. What are you tolerating? What needs to change? What's calling you? What's stopping you? What decisions are you making or not making? What does your version of success look like?

Honour Your Path. Don't make the mistake of thinking you're alone on your path.

The universe has a hand in everything; your successes and your failures!

When you commit to and honour your path, the universe will do the same, and in my view there's no other partner as powerful as the universe to have on your side.

I encourage you to send a signal to the universe today by scheduling a free Path Alignment Strategy Session with me. You can simply email support@shivanibhagi.com or book a time on my appointment calendar at http://www.connectwithshivani.com/.

To your success!

ABOUT SHIVANI BHAGI

Shivani Bhagi is an international Career Success Coach and the host of the Careers Redefined Podcast show.

After 15 years working as a corporate professional, Shivani realised she wanted more for her career and life and decided to take a bold step. In 2010 she packed up everything she had and left her job and home in London to pursue her dreams in Goa, India of a life filled with freedom and sun.

Shivani's mission is to help other professionals around the world forge meaningful and impactful careers so they too can live life on their terms.

As a master facilitator, Shivani has conducted over 300 Leadership workshops for managers in Fortune 500 organisations. She's deeply passionate about mentoring women to take bold steps in their careers and lives and facilitates powerful transformation via her programmes and international retreats.

Shivani's work has been regularly featured in The Huffington Post, Thrive Global and she's soon to appear for an interview on FOX TV.

SHANNON TRAN

START YOUR DAY WITH VISION

"The only thing worse than being blind is having sight but no vision." – Helen Keller

We live in an age of distraction. We are often distracted and unfocused because we are bombarded by information and conflicting messages from social media and society on a daily basis. According to Psychology Today, the average American sees or hears over 4,000 ads per day!

Distraction keeps you scattered and unfocused. This is why Helen Keller's quote is so powerful. Do you lack a clear vision for your life? Are you constantly spinning your wheels and struggling to slow down and relax?

Before I learned how to operate from a clear picture of who I wanted to be and what I wanted to accomplish each day, my life was frantic. I rushed from task to task with no clear intention or purpose. I was exhausted, overworked and burned out. I was overworking myself but not really getting ahead in a meaningful way. Even though I was successful on the outside, I was insecure and weighed down by self-doubt, a critical self-talk, and found it difficult to relax. There was no time for myself.

Once I learned the success principle of "leading with vision" I became free of negative thinking, released negative comparisons, focused on my strengths instead of my weaknesses, and started each day with a routine that supported my well-being. More importantly, I became free of other people's expectations and versions of success. I established my own self-authority.

A coherent vision is a powerful way to promote your success because it increases your productivity, improves your flow, reduces wrong choices and actions, and allows for better time management.

What would your ideal life look like if you operated with a vision? What would your daily schedule look like? How would you start your day? How many hours would you be working? What would you be doing? What would you NOT be doing? Create a picture in your mind and then write down your answer. Also consider what needs to be done to generate and sustain this vision?

According to the Merriam-Webster Dictionary, a vision is defined as "the ability to see; something that you see or dream." A vision statement is an aspirational description of what your ideal life would look and feel like on a daily basis. It serves as a clear guide for choosing current and future courses of action.

A vision tells you where to invest your daily energy. It keeps you accountable because you can quickly see when you're thinking, choices, attitudes, or behaviors are not in alignment. You can course correct in real time.

To create a clear vision for your life, you must consider all the important aspects of your life. These include health, family, career, friendships, fun time and spirituality. Develop a clear vision for each area of your life and include how it will feel to live it.

When I went through this powerful process with my client, Mike, he identified the following vision:

"I know where to invest my energy in order to secure financial freedom, and subsequently personal freedom. Meaning that my house is paid off, my car is paid off, I have at least 10 million in the bank with all taxes paid. I know how to proceed with my hope to change the world and make life better for everyone. I am able to encourage those that I love to become involved. I run several companies that are self-sustaining and employ happy, energetic, tenacious and able people serving a variety of fields such as health, education, life enrichment, home, products, mentoring, work products, and conservation of plan resources. Profits which will remain with employees. I am able to determine how best to encourage and help build lasting foundations for my kids. I am involved in many multi-cultural awareness activities. I have regular meetings with mentors whom I look up to and can trust. I have improved playing guitar, piano and singing. I am physically fit and in the shape I desire."

It took Mike just a few hours to come up with this vision, but it will take him years to build it. A vision develops daily, not in a day. If you want to have a vision that lasts, you must know where to invest your energy on a daily basis. Every day you must ask yourself if what you are doing is moving you closer to that vision. In your vision, you must also consider the people in it. Who do you see in your life? How do you interact with them? Do the people in your life support your vision? Do they bring out the best in you?

You become like the people you spend the most time with. Pay attention to the quality of your relationships. Keep your vision alive by spending time with people who elevate you and inspire you to grow into a better person.

Reduce time with people who are negative, complain, blame, avoid the truth or engage in gossip.

My client, Cindy, realized that she did not have good role models growing up. She wanted to be a better parent to her children than her parents were to her growing up. She created a "family vision" to support her intention and guide her on a daily basis. Here is her vision.

"We have a happy and harmonious home life. We work together as a team to keep our home environment happy and healthy. I am able to find time to unwind each day. We are all mutually responsible for doing our part to make one another feel loved and appreciated. We each nurture our relationships with one another's feelings. We are able to communicate clearly in a respectful manner. We are financially secure, always making more than we spend. We start each day with positivity and motivation. We end each day with honor. We remain patient and kind with one another. We support each other's dreams and aspirations. We put ourselves and each other as first and foremost in all of our life's plans. We thrive as individuals and as a family. We love ourselves and we treat ourselves well so that we can be a positive role model to others."

As you develop your own vision, consider what choices you will no longer make. What behaviors will you no longer tolerate? What situations will you avoid? What emotions and feelings will you no longer embrace that will cause you to turn back to your former self?

Action plan: Write down your vision.

Now that you have a vision, read it daily until you have embodied the vision in mind, body, and spirit.

A few years ago, I realized that I could live "smarter instead of harder" by creating a vision for every area of my life. I created a vision of how I wanted to be as a wife, parent, friend and professional. As a parent, my ultimate vision is raising happy, loving and responsible children with whom I can enjoy an adult relationship with for life. With this result in mind, I reverse engineered what I would need to be, do and have in order for this vision to be a reality. I worked with my belief systems, attitudes and behaviors. This shaped how I interacted with my children.

Over time, I started to see my vision materialize in daily life. My children demonstrate responsible behavior by doing chores and homework on their own. They earn an allowance and spend their money wisely. We enjoy quality time at dinner and engage in lively conversations. We take family vacations twice a year and build positive memories.

As the Chinese proverb says, "If your vision is for a year plant wheat. If your vision is for ten years, plant trees. If your vision is for a lifetime, plant people."

According to Andy Stanley, author of Visioneering, there are four parts to a vision:

1. The problem

2. The solution

3. The reason something must be done

4. The reason something must be done NOW

I like to think of vision as a picture. What would you see and how would you feel if you were living a vision led life?

Take whatever time is needed in order to develop a clear picture for yourself.

To spark your imagination and creativity, you may want to start with the phrase, I imagine...

I imagine a person who...

I imagine a family that...

I imagine a career where...

I imagine a company that...

I imagine a marriage in which...

Be sure to engage your head AND heart. Why must your vision be accomplished? What difference will it make for yourself and others? Why should you create this? What happens if you don't accomplish this?

Action plan: Revise your vision. Read it out loud. Notice how you feel. Does it reflect your values and priorities? Does this vision inspire you?

The power of a vision is that it serves as your North Star. It helps you feel focused, self-assured and anchored. It can motivate you when you feel discouraged or scared of the unknown. It makes decision-making easier because you know exactly where to invest your time and energy. It keeps you from trouble and shows you what to avoid. A vision gives you a sense of purpose, passion and fulfillment. A compelling vision becomes something worth fighting for. It is unfortunate that most people live on automatic pilot instead of a personal vision. I believe this is why so many people feel confused, unhappy and lost.

When you create a vision and align your conscious and subconscious beliefs with it, you will be unstoppable! You will experience FLOW on a regular basis. During challenging times, you will recognize and accept the path you have chosen because you trust yourself. You won't have a major "insecurity issue" or act out in order to get people's approval. More importantly, you will be loved for WHO you are, and not just what you do.

Powerful Visioning Exercise

Imagine that it's a full year from today and you have been on the path to being your best and releasing the problem that kept you stuck. You now have space to BE who you love, DO what you love and HAVE what you love.

Feel where you are right now. Take a deep breath. This is what you notice. Every goal that you have set for yourself this year has been accomplished. You have fulfilled your goals. Some were little, others were things you never imagined you could achieve. You live authentically from your heart in perfect alignment. You are true to yourself. You know yourself as a person who can accomplish whatever goals you set for yourself. What does that feel like? How good does it feel to know that you made all this happen?

Notice what may have surprised you. Notice how over the last year obstacles arose. Things that looked like setbacks arose. At that time, they looked like setbacks and obstacles, but you can see now that what they really did was to assist you. These unexpected experiences course corrected your path so that you could achieve your goals better and faster.

You learned so many valuable lessons along the way that empowered you to move forward faster than before. As you look at your life today, having achieved your intention, look at where and how you live today. What has changed? Who is in your life? What is the quality of your relationships? What do you do with your day? How do you spend your time? How do you feel in your body? How do you feel about your life now knowing what you can do and who you can be?

Notice that you are not the same person as you were 12 months ago. You are more authentic. What needed to shift in order for you to be fully yourself, to be in command of your life? What did you learn about yourself? What do you now say "yes" to and what do you now say "no" to? Remember, every time you say yes to one thing, you are saying no to something else. Every time you say no to something, you are saying yes to something else.

Take notice of anything that seems important to you that came up in the last few minutes. Write it down.

If you are struggling to create a clear and compelling vision for your life, or don't know how to prioritize your life so it's deeply meaningful to you, download your free copy of 7 Productivity Tips for High Achievers at https://shannontranphd.lpages.co/success-rituals/

ABOUT SHANNON TRAN

Dr. Shannon Tran is the founder of Money Mindset Mastery, an online mentoring program for ambitious women who want to experience financial freedom from the inside out. Shannon combines twenty years of knowledge and experience as a team leader in behavior health and a licenced psychologist to equip women to end the struggle with their confidence, value, and worthiness as it relates to money. Dr. Tran combines money mindset with strong personal leadership so you can really step into your confident, worthy self earning what you desire and deserve!

MANIE WALKER

LIFE IS BUT A CHOICE

In the introduction of this book, Gina tells us that what you think and do - day in and day out – is what makes our difference.

Many of us don't realize the root of what we think and do each day is based on the choices we make. Recently, I was studying at Royal Roads University to become a Certified Executive Coach. During that time, I had a discussion with one of my classmates about 'choices'. In essence we both agreed that we all have choices. When we hear someone say, "I have no choice" it sends alarm bells off for us both, because we know everyone has a choice, regardless of their circumstances.

Within this book, Gina has identified women who are conscious of their thoughts and CHOOSE to take ACTION consistently and with purpose. From my perspective, this action is the result of choices you have made, whether you know it or not. With each choice, there are benefits and losses – and choices impact your financial, spiritual, emotional, physical and/or social well-being. And of course, doing nothing is also a choice.

In an extreme example, we can think of Nelson Mandela when he was imprisoned from 1964 to 1982. During his years in prison, Nelson Mandela's reputation grew steadily. He was widely accepted as the most significant black leader in South Africa and became a potent symbol of resistance as the anti-apartheid movement gathered strength. He consistently refused to compromise his political position to obtain his freedom. He made a choice and was willing to pay the price.

In my life, I have made some tough choices, and believe you me; I spent a lot of time and energy in making those choices. With more life experience, I have continued to make choices based on my values – honesty, integrity, fairness, courage, and perseverance. What is different today is my level of self-awareness. Specifically, I now have a better understanding of who I am, as well as my strengths and "triggers". For example a "trigger" for me was my focus on obligations or the expectations of my ancestry.

I am a daughter of Greek-Macedonian parents and being a daughter was in no way equal to being a son in our home. This is the simple truth. Even with my Father being particularly more forward thinking, he at his core, had this belief. I grew up in the hospitality business and started working at the age of 14 as a waitress. It was a great gig and embedded both a strong work ethic and the principles of customer service within me. Before going to University for my first degree, I needed to answer the following question – do I want to work with my Father in the restaurant business? I loved and adored my Father and there was a strong pull, however I made the choice to pursue a career in human resources management. My brother on the other hand, made the decision to partner with my Father in the restaurant business.

I was married at an early age and had two beautiful daughters – Katarina and Ellia – both special and each very different. When Ellia was diagnosed with Autism PDD-NOS, I had a choice to make about the impact this would have on my life and my family. After scanning the landscape and having conversations with many friends and confidants, I made the choice that my daughter Ellia would not define my life. I knew I needed help to take this step, so I sought professional help.

During talk therapy, I learned so many things about myself and how I came to the choices I made up until that point in my life. This led me to another realization. My issue was not my daughter with special needs but instead it was being married to someone that was not the right match for me – on so many different levels. Again, I went back to my process of scanning the landscape and speaking with many friends and confidants. I made the choice to leave the marriage. Some people thought I was just crazy because I had a beautiful home, a handsome and fun husband who provided for his family and two beautiful daughters. When I went back to my values, I realized that although this choice to separate from my husband, would lead to many "bumps" in the road, I knew it was right for me and my daughters.

When I started my human resources consulting business, I was also a single Mom. During this time, there were many choices and in fact there were many "bumps" along the way. Today, when I take time to reflect, I realize that my determination – or just pure grit – allowed me to deal with all the challenges that came my way, however well worth the price I paid.

A friend of mine who recently separated from his wife had delayed this choice for a host of reasons, however at the core was his belief he didn't really have a choice. There was a breaking point and he officially separated from his wife. Six months after this choice, he was off all his medication and his overall state of health was better than it had been for years. Choices we all have to make them and we need to understand the prices (and pluses!) we are willing to take on.

After 12 years in my human resources consulting business, I made the choice to go back to the corporate world. Again, I followed my process of scanning the landscape and speaking with many friends and confidants. I remember signing the offer of employment on Christmas Eve and taking on the role of a Human Resources Business Partner with KPMG in Canada. This professional services firm was a great place to work. I had the privilege of supporting many corporate leaders as they made decisions on the "people side" of the business. I had so many rich and complex conversations. As their trusted advisor, I also presented solutions as choices. There were various solutions within many different dimensions – money, brand, culture, etc. These discussions went on until each corporate leader felt comfortable with their choice and the price involved.

When I made the choice to go back to University in my 50's, I continued to follow my now familiar process of scanning the landscape and having conversations with many friends and confidants. I felt it was time that I gave back to my community and I believed coaching – enabling individuals to focus and move forward on their personal and professional priorities, through the exploration of ideas and candid discussions with a confidential and unbiased thinking partner - would be a great way to finish my career.

With 30 years business experience behind me, some of my friends and confidants thought my plan B might be a better choice, as I had enough grey hair to take on the role of a business coach. My plan B was to go on a six-week European vacation with the money and this was tempting. But I chose Plan A.

Going to Royal Roads University (RRU) and becoming a coach was one of the best choices I have made in my life. I met an outstanding group of people and had an entirely new appreciation for what coaching was really all about. Up until this point, I believed I was a coach to my leaders/clients; however, I only resembled a coach.

As I took time to reflect, I realized the process I had in place - scanning the landscape and having conversations with many friends and confidants – did entail some type of coaching. What did scanning the landscape look like? Many a night was spent on the internet, often with a nice glass of Sauvignon Blanc, to research and learn what were some best practices and lessons learned by others. Once I had this under my belt, I sought input from friends and confidants that I trusted which allowed me to reflect and think about my thinking. At the time, I thought these were just conversations; however, I experienced coaching because I was able to move forward and gain clarity on what was important to me.

Today, as a coach, I am delighted to help others move forward and make choices that are important to them. To that end, I created my mission statement: To connect people to their inner voice - what's personally meaningful and significant - so they can find joy by aligning their life with who they are and what they want to do and have.

I developed this mission statement because of my choice to obtain my Graduate Certificate in Executive Coaching. Coaching is a process that involves integrity, accountability, action and truly understanding what is meaningful to you. We are pulled in many directions and taking the time to focus on you, will impact everyone who you encounter.

In other words, we each have a mission, should we choose to accept it. What is the driving force behind your mission?

That takes me back to my friend from RRU where we had a shared perspective when we heard people say, "I don't have a choice". This drives us both crazy however we now have a coach-approach to be of service to our community and help individuals move forward to gain clarity on what is significant to them, in that moment.

Life is but a choice…

What price are you willing to pay for the choices you make?

And what choices will you make to move forward with your life and your dreams?

Experience the power of coaching with a complimentary 30-minute Next Step Clarity Session.

During your private no-cost session, I'll help you get clear about what you want to happen in your business over the next 90 days and identify an action step so you can immediately activate your plan.

To schedule your session contact me on my website https://targethr.net/ or message me on LinkedIn at https://www.linkedin.com/in/maniewalker.

ABOUT MANIE WALKER

BA, CHRL, CEC, ACC

Drawing on over 30 years of experience, Manie has a passion for the people side of the business and making an impact. As a coach, she creates a safe, inviting and confidential space to serve as a thinking partner and empower each coachee to take action. Manie's values - honesty, integrity, fairness, courage, and perseverance - act as her 'North Star', while pursuing her mission, one coachee at a time.

Manie has a Bachelor of Arts from McMaster University, a CHRL designation from the Human Resources Professional Association of Ontario, a Certificate in Organization Development from Queens University as well as a Graduate Certificate in Executive Coaching, from Royal Roads University. In addition, she has achieved the designation of ACC from the International Coaching Federation (ICF). This career milestone signifies her commitment to high professional and ethical standards in the coaching industry, and to her own continued growth and education clients.

Manie lives in Dundas, Ontario, Canada with her husband and their blended family. She is a Toronto Maple Leaf fan and has been a beginner golfer for years.

MANIE WALKER

EDITH UNDERWOOD

LIVING MINDFULLY THROUGH LIFE-CHANGING MOMENTS

Can you think of "one big moment," a turning point that changed your life and radically altered the path you were on? These are the moments when your destiny is shaped.

My turning-point moment was a phone call. The days that followed marked the beginning of a downward spiral fueled by business and financial loss for myself and my partner as we began to see our successful corporation disappear in front of our eyes. Just a few years before, we had been on an absolute high living the lifestyle we designed.

During that call, we lost a brand we had focused all our time, energy and resources on. Our distribution company introduces new brands to the market with exclusive distribution rights. And in that moment, we learned how fast the ups can become downs and that we needed to reframe to stay on a positive path.

It was the beginning of a new era for us.

I've learned that you can't fully experience the high points of your journey without the contrast of the lows.

As a business owner and educator, I am often faced with challenging situations that need high levels of flexibility and creative solutions to foster growth.

Life is like that. We have expectations of how we think life should unfold and we approach our lives through the lens of these expectations. And then, when a gigantic detour presents itself, sometimes life feels like a highway with very few exits, and in order to regain that passion for the life you want, you must recover ownership of your choices.

I've learned that dropping expectations and adapting to the unfolding of life however it reveals itself, will set you free. How you respond to challenges and unexpected turns is the way you can begin to shape your destiny.

In business it is not about the ideas, everyone has ideas, it is about the executions of these ideas and the willingness to outwork and outlearn everyone on your path. When life presents itself as a highway with few exits, will you spend the entire time looking for that exit or a way back to where you used to be, to your comfort zone? Or will you move forward choosing to enjoy the scenery along the way?

My partner and I learned some deep lessons the last few years. When you find yourself in a negative cycle, you must break the pattern. I've gained some important insight about risk-taking in this process. I realized that when we come from nothing, we have nothing to lose. This mindset first helped us achieve success in the real estate world, and ultimately led to success in our distribution ventures.

Life is a flow of ups and downs.

All experiences are opportunities for growth, personal or professional, good or bad. For me, mindfulness has become an essential strategy to mitigate business-related stress and this new way of life quickly became my number one success ritual.

A big part of this mindfulness practice is to watch your "reaction" to what is unfolding. The experience of an enormous loss about an unknown future is unsettling, but I am now in a different place and this cultivates a different response. Unexpected turns and heightened stress are often present in business. And if we live this experience from a fight or flight mode, we operate from a zone of reactivity. We might even believe that it is 'normal'. There is nothing 'normal' about stress! It's not your natural state of being.

Mindfulness has allowed me to cultivate the practice of meditation, self-reflection, stillness, and helps me act from non-reactivity. It has allowed me to step back and learn to see the 'outer reality' clearly. I've learned how transient it can be and how important it is to notice how you are showing up in everyday life.

When life shifts you out of your comfort zone growth can take place, teaching you to adapt quickly and think on your feet. Most importantly it allows you to step back and reframe the story with a new translation of what is happening.

I've come to believe that growing your consciousness is a requirement of scaling your business in today's world. Meditation is like consciously spending time with yourself. When we learn to manage what is happening inside ourselves, we are better equipped to manage what is happening to and around us.

Getting refocused and centered again happens faster when you spend time with yourself. I have become highly conscious about my morning routine and make sure I spend time with myself and follow a consistent morning practice. This became my success ritual. Spending time with oneself intentionally and consistently unfolds as a meditation practice

We know that it is important to scale a business but it is just as important to scale ourselves. If you don't take time to scale yourself how will you handle the pressures of growing a business. Constantly feeling that you need to meet certain expectations will create a tremendous amount of stress. Mindfulness is non-judgmental. What makes mindfulness so unique is that everyone can do it. It is not something that we have to learn, but rather a way of being and thinking that brings us more in touch with what is happening in the now. It allows us to become less restrained by the past, our habits, expectations or assumptions, and more able to respond to events as they unfold, with an open mind and an open heart.

Meditation is the process of getting to know and understand the energy that is constantly flowing through us, and learning how to harness this energy so we are intentionally investing this energy throughout the day. This way Meditation becomes intentionally working with the energy that flows through us.

Meditation helps you learn how to harness that energy, and concentrate on a single point of focus with a clear process and a goal. It is very important to note that meditation is not about emptying your mind, it's not about clearing your mind. It is about focusing your mind, and arriving at an extremely concentrated state. The more focused you are the better you are in utilizing your time and energy.

With focus comes clarity. As opportunities arise you need to see if they align with your purpose. If they don't align don't take them. This way the opportunity won't become a distraction.

I recommend following a 3 step plan when implementing a mindfulness practice to your success rituals.

Step 1. Understand where your awareness goes

It takes practice to understand we can control where our awareness goes. I recommend a daily meditation practice and I recommend you to start slow. Set your time and place and be consistent. I prefer to meditate first thing in the morning as setting my intentions for the day, but many people also enjoy meditating before bedtime. Whatever you prefer set into a daily routine and commit to consistency. It is good to practice at the same time and place each day. Routine is the best tool for training your mind. Start small. Ten minutes a day is a great beginning but often I recommend my clients to start with 3 minutes each day. If you find this intimidating, you may start by taking just 5 breaths each day and slowly working your way up to 10 minutes. I have detailed guided practices on my website to help you get going. Once you establish a regular 10 minutes daily you can think about extending this practice. Tip: Observe your breath. This means you will simply focus on your breathing while you meditate.

Step 2. Increase your focus with mindfulness

Being able to concentrate is imperative to your mindfulness practice. First, you learn it then you practice it. My master teacher Dandapani often says if you want to become good at concentration you actually have to practice it every day, the way you would practice playing the piano every day if you want to be a great player. Concentration itself needs to become part of your daily life. Start by paying undivided attention to your loved ones daily. "Giving someone your undivided attention is one of the highest forms of love and respect that you can express to them." Dandapani

Another great way to increase focus happens during mediations. As you are observing your breathing you may want to repeat "breathing in" "breathing out" as you are focusing on your in-and-out breath. This concentration technique helps you focus on one point.

Step 3. Positively invest your energy

If I invest my energy into something positive it will grow and become more positive. If I invest my energy in something negative it will grow and become more negative. Think about the negative challenges you had to face with your business or personal life. When a challenge presents itself, you need to see how you can translate the story and reframe the situation to flip it into a positive outcome. When you invest your energy into positive behaviour it will start to grow and manifest positive reactions in your life.

Cultivating a mindfulness practice will be your tool to check in on your habitual conditioning and use every opportunity whether it be situations, or people, as an entry point for your growth.

The path is a simple one, but the mind is devious and conditioned. The mind will absolutely take you away from something which will bring you peace because it's very nature is a disturbance. It will put a chatter in your head to attempt to sabotage your peace and rob you of the moment. I learned that although our mind desperately tries to leave trauma or toxic stress behind, our bodies keep the scores. They keep us trapped in the past with wordless emotions and feelings. This is what spirals into inner disconnections and creates annihilation of marriages, families, and friendships.

What stuck to me is the realization that no one goes to a doctor when they are well. But we do try our best to maintain our body regularly. That's the purpose of cultivating a deep sustainable Mindfulness practice.

We are not cultivating a practice because our expectation of life is to flow smoothly, rather we need to cultivate the practice when we are struggling from the strong winds of change and are closer to dawn.

"You can't stop the waves but you can learn to surf" is one of my mantras from Joh Kabat-Zinn. He showed me that the purpose of cultivating a mindfulness practice is to build a strong enough ship of wisdom to guide us through hard times and calm times.

When I received that life-changing phone call I came to understand a key concept in mindfulness meditation: Impermanence. Everything is constantly changing; nothing is fixed or certain.

If I think about where we needed to go with our business that call was part of an opening to get there. And the truth is, the law of impermanence is very freeing because it reminds us that we don't have to hold onto things so tightly since everything comes and goes.

From this new level of awareness, I was able to take a step back and reframe our situation so we could quickly start moving forward in a positive, new direction. It allowed me to let go and flow with the changes in my life instead of fighting them.

This is how mindfulness changed our lives.

Reconnecting your thoughts with your body to experience mindfulness meditation is the first step on a life-changing and enriching journey. You are welcome to begin this journey on your own by working through my self-directed online courses at www.edithunderwood.com or by exploring the free online tools available there. Additionally, as a complement to The Success Ritual readers you are welcome to schedule a FREE call with me to discuss your goals.

One's mindfulness journey cannot be complete without the proper tools to further support you as you grow. One vital tool I recommend for all beginners is the Self-Care Wheel, which is another free resource waiting for you on my site. To get to where you want to go, you need to know where you currently are. The Self Care Wheel is a simple, yet effective diagnostic tool to help give you a powerful visual representation of all areas of your Self Care regimen and how they relate to one another. It gives you a snapshot of where you are right now, which will help shine a spotlight on the areas that need immediate attention to help you manage every-day stress, and increase contentment and life satisfaction.

Tools can also be used to bring mindfulness home for your children. By implementing a Peace Corner in your home you can start raising mindful beings with our specially designed yoga mats and mindfulness activities for children. All kids need a calming space that can foster an environment for more learning and self-discovery through child led meditations, the earlier these mindful habits start the better.

Life changing moments can either be our worst enemies or greatest allies. These moments are crossroads in life. You can react or respond, the choice will always be within your power and it is in that moment of decisions, when your destiny is shaped.

What is your story?

Can you capitalize on everyday twists and turns in life and use life's flow to your advantage?

Only you can guide yourself around this and transform even the lowest points in your story to support your future success.

ABOUT EDITH UNDERWOOD

Edith is a mother, educator, author, teacher trainer and business owner. Above all she is a Mindfulness Meditation. She practices in Mississauga, Canada, as well as online; running mindfulness courses and groups for individuals and businesses who are looking for a non-judgmental tool to help guide them through overwhelming feelings and challenges.

Mindfulness and meditation have made deep inroads into the corporate world. Her approach of using mindfulness provides clients with the necessary tools to handle everyday stresses allowing them to reflect effectively, focus sharply on the task at hand, master peak levels of stress, and recharge quickly.

Edith runs a successful distribution company with her husband and after introducing many trendy brands to the North American market the couple launched their own brand Brean an eco-conscious, sustainable, practical lifestyle brand dedicated to quality and modern style. Edith is also the owner of The Peace Corner, @peacecornerco and Brean @breanworld, www.breanworld.com

EDITH UNDERWOOD

MICHELINE EDWARDS

CREATE SPACE FOR SUCCESS WITH SAFE EXPOSURE

"Awe little birds you were created to sing and you are singing…."

So begins one of my favorite quotes. This quote belongs to St. John Vianney the Cure of Ares (1786-1859). The quote continues; "man was created to love God and yet…." I love this quote on a spiritual level but also as a reminder that in life that we are all created to do something.

What are you called to do?

Identifying who we are; our ambitions and what we need to thrive, is so immensely important to our success and happiness. But many of us don't realize our callings: simple or elaborate. So what is it that keeps us from living vibrantly and realizing our full potential.

Most of us have had a dream about being naked in a public setting. Usually our clothes cover our bodies and things we don't wish to show others without granting them permission. Exposing what we hold as private can be unnerving especially in unfamiliar space. What do you keep hidden from yourself and others?

Why is exposure of our needs, wants and our most true self so hard? Sharing our inner self can often be as uncomfortable as having a body image issue we couldn't cover up. Putting yourself out there can be hard. Placing your dreams out in the public eye to either sink or swim can be quite an obstacle for the female entrepreneur. When you add in the "critical self", guilt and social judgement issues that many women encounter daily; being successful in life let alone business, can be daunting.

Defining, achieving, and recognizing success is a different path for every person. There are four key elements I found to be crucial to my success as a human being and female entrepreneur. These four elements became my pass to resiliency and happiness in life no matter what I was faced with. Creating a ritual of always knowing these four things will allow you to tackle whatever life throws at you and to do most anything your heart desires with ease and grace.

1. Know who you (honestly) are?

2. Take the time to define your idea of what a boundary is and what it should be for you to thrive?

3. Have an honest inner dialogue with yourself; how willing are you to change or adapt as needed (what are areas of compromise and no compromise)?

4. What will create and hold a space for you to allow defining moments to happen?

All four of these elements are ever changing and require being open to honestly redefining what these are for you regularly.

Let's start with: Who are you?

Most of us define ourselves by the external labels and visual caps we wear. Our gender, marital status, our children or lack of, our occupation, our spouse's occupation, and our age; even what we think others want to hear. Typically, when a client defines who she is to me at a first session it is something like this:

"Hi I am Mary, I am married to Bob and we have 3 children. I am a part time nurse. I had eggs for breakfast and spent most of my time running kids around. My hobbies used to be collecting socks and bathing but now I don't have time. I might like to feel human someday but I'm not really sure."

These responses make me sad and usually so is Mary. The other typical response is this:

"My name is Mary and I've been married to Bob for 16 yrs. We have 3 kids. I have a dream of doing XXXXX but I'm not really sure what I want to do OR if my idea is dumb OR if I can do this with all my other responsibilities. I guess someday I'll be able too."

Both of these responses are followed up with me saying, "Great but who are you and what makes you sparkle?" Usually the word sparkle gets a giggle or no acknowledgment. A timid answer follows:

"Well I've told you about everything I could think of."

As a person, if you don't have a clear idea of who you are without applying labels, you are lost in a sea of nothing.

To move forward you need to be able to "expose" & define who you are at your very core before society, family, friends, kids and the world defined this for you.

Do you remember who you were when nobody created an image for you? Maybe you do or maybe you don't; one of the most key elements to moving forward and being successful is knowing who you are and being comfortable with who that is. If you are unable to recognize, be honest and transparent with yourself about your inner dreams, desires, needs and beliefs: nobody else can (for you) define, establish or support you. How can you expect to live a life that moves in a direction you desire when," you don't know who you truly are"? So figure out who you are. Once you know who you are, it is easier to let others know your direction in life and to follow through with what you desire. Positive change in you cannot occur until you offer transparency. Grab a pen and paper or journal and explore: Who are you really?

My next question for your consideration is: What is your idea of a boundary? Further, do you have boundaries? And, if you do, are they working for you?

Boundaries according to Merriam Webster are "ceilings, caps, confines, ends, limitations, a line, or termination". When I read these aloud, I think of "Brick walls". Brick is great; it is solid and stands the test of time. It is hard to see over or around. It doesn't shift or mold itself easily and it is hard to move.

Our modern society has put boundaries on a pedestal: without creating a clear way of establishing their structure and when they need to be adjusted or removed. The defining words from Merriam Webster, elicit a sense of end, doom, closure and staying hidden or not moving forward: almost as if danger lurks. While some people think they are creating boundaries as a safe space; most people are actually building impenetrable brick walls. These walls cannot be seen around or over; nor can they be easily shifted or opened if opportunities present themselves.

I prefer to define boundaries as;

"unofficial rules or limits that define an acceptable behavior".

Boundaries should be part of an ever-changing process that aligns with your values, needs, goals (who you are). Boundaries should be "Gated Fences" or even better a "Gated Community" that you choose to openly live within. You allow things to come and go safely as they serve who you are. A gated fence is easier to adjust, open, close or even add gates as you need them.

Now take this definition a step further, as a "Gated Community" you identify and invite in those people and things that support you in creating success and joy. You get to select who (or what) builds you up, moves you forward and holds continued respect for your space. You own this space; it is easier to see what is on the other side. You are able to react positively not defensively when you can see what is coming at you. Having a clear view from a safe area allows you to be more welcoming of approaching opportunity as well.

Boundaries are the terms which you feel define acceptable behavior. Acceptable behavior is not just what you will tolerate or accept but that which holds space for your morals, values, and personal growth. It is not carved in stone and can be evolving according to your ideals. Acceptable behavior does not infringe on the personal space or values of another.

When building your gated community take pride in and embellish this space with your essence. This is your way of communicating to the world that you are proud of your goals, know who you are, have self-respect and worth and will not allow someone/thing else to define you. Boundaries are not to keep things out but for you to select what comes in. What flows freely through your gates should be a vision of who you are and what is supportive of you (no more naked vulnerability).

To create a gated community, you may also need to "survey" boundaries that were not serving you or were nonexistent, as well as new guidelines for your gated fence. Take some time or write out what your past boundaries have been (or not been), issues you had with them and what you desire them to be. This is very unsettling for many women as they often realize they have either created brick walls or no boundaries at all. Often you believe your community is in order, yet your life is in shambles. As you break down where you are and begin to build your fence a section at a time according to who you really are; truer visions begin to appear. You need to be open to changes as things come to the surface. You may need to change your behaviors, reactions and responses. Rebuild your gated community according to who you really are: not what you feel others have defined for you.

Many of us become people pleasers. We lose our sense of direction and self. We place ourselves at a disadvantage while trying to accommodate everyone. The initial act of always putting everyone else first creates a (sense of) high. Later when you come down from this you feel; unappreciated, tired, used up, as if you as a person and your goals don't matter. Many women I work with make a habit of people pleasing. In trying to do the right thing, they eventually become resentful or lose their own self-worth because they give so much they forget how to RECEIVE (take note that self care is an act of receiving). Learning to balance giving and receiving is crucial to having a community that has "checks & balance" thus building gratitude and joy.

I believe a certain amount of selfishness is necessary to create healthy boundaries. Turning people away is a tough thing to do especially if they have rebuttals for your reasons. Do not give reasons. You don't owe anyone this and it leads to compromises or situations you will later resent. Learning to say "NO" is a very wise choice when what is being asked compromises who you are or your gated community.

Recognizing that you need and have the right to certain things; is essential to creating a sacred and personal gated space.

You have a need and a right to: Say NO, to have others respect your space, to have your choices respected even if those around you do not always agree. You have a right to identify individuals, actions or behaviors you find unacceptable and remove yourself from these. You have a right to trust in and believe in yourself. You not only have this last right; but you need to nurture it and hold it dear. You have a right to ask for respect for your dreams, space, quiet time and for others even within the family to respect this.

Creating a gated fence or community for yourself can be trying when you begin. Often those you hold close will not be accepting of your new fence. It is a lot like fencing in your backyard. Some neighbors might not like it. It is good to remember that those who throw the biggest fuss about your new gated fence or community (boundaries) are those who were benefiting the most from you not having a fence.

Know who you are, establish a gated community and be willing to adjust or change old habits but not compromise your core values. Be honest with yourself and others about where you are and what you are willing to offer (not can), this can be humbling. Be thankful for what you do have and understanding of where you need to build or change.

After you know who you are and what your career and life goals are, your gated community will create and hold space for you to move forward with fewer obstacles. You will be more aware of what you want and need and be ultimately more prepared for obstacles that pop up. Being able to decide calmly and assertively according to what you have established (during a well thought out process) serves you more effectively. You won't feel as though you have made compromises that don't align with your direction causing you to become frustrated or give up what you are working for. Additionally, your safe space will prevent you from feeling cornered, used, tired and over committed. And, you will see more space opening in your life which will facilitate being able to seize more of opportunities that serve you.

I encourage you to expose yourself, offer maximum transparency and honesty to yourself and to others. People are not mind readers and even if they were, your mind must be true to self-first. When you do this, it may feel a bit like you are standing naked in a crowd. You may feel anxiety admitting who you really are to yourself and even more so to others. You might be afraid: do it anyway. This will be hard in the beginning, training yourself to rely on your gated community. Your community will support you and your dreams. The more you learn to open and close the gate to your chosen community; you free yourself and achieve your goals become something of ease and grace in your life. Exposure in a community of support will be the beginning of some of your most defining moments!

I am overjoyed that you joined me and all the fabulous authors in The Success Rituals. I hope you find yourself inspired by our book.

I so enjoyed sharing my chapter about healthy boundaries, what they look like and how to establish the basics and begin the process of making this work for you. If you are interested in diving deeper into this topic to discover at a more intimate level how to provide transparency and apply it to build your own "gated community".

As a thank you and to take you on your next step in designing a life you love and to learn more about starting your own "safe exposure community (space)", I would love to offer you an exclusive gift just for the readers of our book.

You can find your next step to begin your journey to a #ridiculouslyamazinglife at

www.michelineedwards.com/SuccessRitualsGift

And, I invite you to visit my website http://www.michelineedwards.com/ to explore the possibilities in your life #imaginethepossibilities

Please also connect and follow me on Instagram and LinkedIn @michelineedwards, and on Facebook @MichelineTransformationalCoach

ABOUT MICHELINE EDWARDS

As a Life & Health Coach, Micheline has been changing lives for over 25 years.

Micheline is a retired Midwife, Doula (charter member of DONA), L.C. and a Parent/Family Educator who has guided hundreds of women through some of their most intimate transitions in life.

She is the Founder & Creator of Your Life Code of Rights, a coaching platform developed from her experience as a labor and delivery provider.

She is a wife of 30 years, mother to five children and an ever-growing nest of grandchildren. She enjoys public speaking and is a Certified Bars Facilitator and Reiki Master.

Her passion for life leads her to embrace every moment with celebration & guide her clients to do the same.

MICHELINE EDWARDS

ALICIA FAITH

SPIRITUAL HYGIENE

Mystics are everywhere and they are successful AF!!

When YOU hear the word mystic who comes to the front of your mind?

The Palm reader down the road? Your friend reading your tarot cards online? Mmhmm... or...how about the lady who owned your favorite boutique or bakery, and what about the chiropractor you went to last week? Yes even your sweet aunt with her quilt shop online is a mystic.

You see a MYSTIC is simply one who sees! We see magic everywhere! We see depth! We see lack. We see love! But mostly we see your TRUTH that lies dormant beyond what is generally accepted as intellect in today's society and we seek harmony with all of nature and the universe!

Mystics are the ones who work with energy unseen. Ones who embrace their spirituality as infinite wisdom, as intuition set afire. And we use this in our daily tasks, decisions, and routines.

YOU have all these capabilities too! You only need to acknowledge your potential and choose to see!

An ENTREPRENEUR MYSTIC is someone who has translated this innate knowledge from universal energies, (Often experienced and referred to as the Divine, Spirit, Source and/or God.) into tangible forms of currency. We create an outlet for our energy + time and exchange that for the currency of our liking. Could be cash, could mean bartering for something even better.

But the SUCCESSFUL ENTREPRENEUR MYSTIC is that among us who knows the biggest factor to achieving their goals and reaching their dream is maintaining our spiritual hygiene throughout the various stages of this exchange (energy to currency).

We recognize the significance of health and wellness in not only the physical body, but our spirit bodies as well. We work on our spiritual health similarly to the way you'd think of brushing your hair or cleaning under your fingernails. Some of it is easy and daily. Some of it requires we dig a little deeper on an as needed basis, similarly to the way we might need a chiropractic adjustment from time to time, or dental cleaning.

Then there's the things we do that have such a significant impact on how we identify with ourselves and others that it's only necessary once in our lifetime, maybe you had braces to improve our dental health for a period of your life.

We also have spiritual practices that profoundly assist in transcending us to a new level of spiritual understanding and integration.

It is first important to understand that our physical bodies can hide our lack of spiritual health for quite some time, but eventually it shows its ugly head like a festering pimple on prom night!

Let me ask you a question. Have you ever run into someone and had a wonderful conversation but still walked away confused and scratching your head? Not quite able to put your finger on it, but something was just off, unsure why or what, but definitely off. That feeling... the uneasiness... that was the imbalance of the physical and spiritual bodies within that person. These combatting frequencies make it very difficult for another person to tune into. Imagine how that could feel from the business aspect.

I guarantee your customers and clientele feel that as well. While no one is expecting perfection... your clients are at the very least looking for consistency. Consistency and integrity of who you are in person and in business. So it is imperative we focus just as much, if not more, on our Spiritual Hygiene as we do our physical.

One of the most important things we can do for ourselves as well as within our business is to learn how to address our shadow selves. You know those little insecure voices that keep us playing small, yeah, those guys.

To be successful, we must be willing to take a good long hard look at those pieces of ourselves and nurture them back to health! To do this we must learn to navigate our energy + emotions (aka spirit + body) and begin routines of spiritual hygiene.

When we are conscious and aware of what is going on with our energetic/ spiritual selves, the other areas of our lives will certainly feel the effects of these practices especially... you guessed it...in your BUSINESS! I can tell you from personal experiences, your customers will feel when you are not energetically/ spiritually aligned with your offers, services, and products, and it could end up costing you greatly. Maybe it already has... but we can fix that!! Let's look at a few ways to be sure your business is in alignment and integrity with who you are.

Some mystics like to stick to a usual ritual routine where they celebrate, observe and cleanse themselves, their spaces, and their tools with the cycle of the moon or on the 1st of every month for example. For others, they may wait until they experience symptoms that show it is time to work on some spiritual hygiene for themselves, their energy, or their business. I prefer to dabble in hygienic rituals daily and add "a la carte" style when symptoms or situations arise.

We care for our teeth daily, we care for our skin daily. Then, it begs to reason that we could also be benefiting by tending to our spiritual bodies in a similar manner.

For the daily care of our spiritual side can be seen as using essential oils (both topically and in a diffuser), performing self care Reiki, becoming familiar with our shadow selves, nurturing our inner child (after all she's the one with all the dreams and aspirations!) and tuning into the depths of our intuition. Commitment to spiritual hygiene only takes a short time to ignite your gifts! In turn expanding and growing your business in the most personal, profound and unique way.

I suggest trying Frankincense and Orange for awakening your intuitive intentions and creative inner child and see what emerges! Grab a notebook and allow the ideas to flow and embrace your sacred wisdom! A quick internet search will blow your mind at the amazing beneficial properties for mind, body and spirit found in both of these delicious essential oils! Or reach out to me for information and a sample!

It matters not whether your business is run from a busy office downtown or at home between kid runs. These tips aren't specific to online businesses or the good ole brick n mortar type. Nurturing and maintaining the spiritual hygiene and energy that surrounds you and your business will take any business model to its next level.

Also know that no matter how long you've been an entrepreneur, whether it be 3 months or 30 years, whether you had one transaction or a 1000 transactions, we all have had those experiences in life that left us exasperated and desperately wishing for the power to read minds!!

Well, that's not completely outside the realm of possibilities? I help people learn to do this every day! Everyone has the ability just waiting to be tapped into.

I want to show you how focusing these abilities in your entrepreneurial escapades can lead you down some very successful paths not just in your personal life but in business.

If you could learn to read people and anticipate their needs... just imagine the significant impact on every aspect of life.... Now I'm not necessarily talking about late night psychics and fortune tellers I'm talking more about intuition and your innate womanly knowledge.

If I could give you a couple of rituals to practice that would increase your ability to tap into your customers deepest desires, wouldn't you want to give it a solid run at developing these Success Rituals for the spirit? I use my gifts to help women develop their own ability to anticipate their customers and client's deepest desires, even before their clients know what they want, and I can help you do the same!

Now you might roll your eyes at the idea of a psychic: but allow me to explain. What we are about to discuss might just change your perspective.

You see every single one of us has this natural ability buried within our genetics. Your DNA is so much more magical than anyone ever taught you in school. And with knowledge, and a wee bit of practice, we can easily tap into these gifts and expand them into what may appear to some as a supernatural power. Reading people and understanding their needs becomes as instinctual as breathing.

I'd like to shed some light on the spiritual aspects of entrepreneurship, and help you develop rituals that will blow the roof off your business!

Imagine the realtor being able to personally select more houses and more ecstatic faces when clients are amazed and astounded and exclaim "how did you know?!" And the fashion designer who always hits the new trends! What about the hairdresser, the motorcycle tech, the teacher, and the doctors?!

Can we please take a moment to appreciate the implication of developing more Successful MYSTIC Entrepreneurs! Like wow! I am here for that! I am here for all of that!!

As a DNA ReActivation Practitioner, I utilize light language, Reiki, meditation and various energy healing techniques to repair and reactivate those DNA strands in you to assist the expansion of your abilities! Through this work you can ignite a source of knowledge for you to continue a healthy spiritual journey that is true to YOU and, when you are in alignment, your business easily falls into place and you begin to blossom! It's THE MOST eye opening once in a lifetime experience every entrepreneur needs! Your activation is permanent, your spiritual gifts are yours to keep and use to grow and prosper in body and in business!

Reach out to me if you need clarity on your soul's mission or how to get back on track. I will help steer your business into a direction that lights you on fire and resonates with your spirit! And then I'll help you establish clear lines of communication with the energies of love and abundance from the universe!

I want to help every female entrepreneur recognize their mystic side and become hella successful! If that's you and you're ready to have 48 strands of lit up DNA radiating success, done in 4, 60 to 90 minute sessions, I will give you the first session FREE! Do not wait! Your clientele needs you! Your dreams need you!

You can find me across most social media platforms as Alicia Faith, The Barefoot Mystic!! https://linktr.ee/Barefoot.Mystic or you can email me directly at transcendaf@gmail.com

AND you are warmly invited to join our virtual oasis on Facebook https://www.facebook.com/groups/TranscendSociety - a growing community of mystical women supporting each other with tips, hacks, memes and encouraging words of Spiritual health and transcendence!

ABOUT ALICIA FAITH

Mystics are everywhere, you only have to acknowledge your potential and choose to see.

Alicia Faith is a natural born clairsentient, clairvoyant, empath and medium, who burst out of the "broom closet" in the autumn of 2017 to show herself and the world what she was made of!! And she is here to help women entrepreneurs, like YOU, find their way out of their own!

Alicia will bring the best out in you and your business by assisting you with recognizing and expanding your gifts for the purpose of professional and personal growth!

You are magic af!! Come on out and play!!

RHIANNON TARRANT

FLIP THE SCRIPT

Living fiercely true to your potential requires that you learn how to master high powered performance, aka, the consistent, meaningful output that helps you excel.

Despite understanding this concept intellectually, I found that I was, along with many other ambitious, self-making women, struggling to sustain high powered performance. I would experience intermittent bursts of powerful output but then something would happen to knock me off my game and I'd lose the upward momentum and critical traction I'd created for myself.

In the midst of a particularly rough patch where I had been plagued by all kinds of 'performance blockers', I realized that if I couldn't figure out how to get - and stay - in that high performance sweet spot, I'd never actually take my game to the next level and I'd never capitalize on my potential. Since succumbing to mediocrity is one of my greatest fears, I set out on a mission to figure out where - and why - my high performance obstacles existed and how I could override and replace these limitations with rinse-and-repeat systems that made consistent high powered performance a no-brainer.

I'm happy to report that the mission was a success. It resulted in the guiding philosophy (Flip the Script) and the 4 Pillar framework of High Powered Performance that I used to pull me out of an eight month slump, launch an elevated branch of my coaching business and start making critical moves that I had previously been too consumed by fear and self-doubt to make. Combined, Flip the Script and my 4 Pillars have become the effective approach that both my students and I continue to use as we take our success to the next level and it's what I'm going to share with you here in this book so that you too, can smash past your limits and start playing big.

"Flip the Script"

Identifying the obstacles to consistent, High Powered Performance is one thing but understanding why those obstacles exist in the first place is, in my opinion, far more important. As I started to dig into this query, I realized that all of our hang ups - the things that have been keeping our game small - are the result of societal conditioning; the limiting conventions and expectations that we've absorbed and believe to be truths.

For example, women are socialized to believe that we should be everything and do everything - for everyone. We're socialized to believe that not only are we "supposed" to do it all, but that we're supposed to do it all perfectly and look "perfect" while doing it. We're socialized to believe that everyone else's needs should come before our own and that prioritizing ourselves is selfish, that going along is good and that stepping up and speaking out is bad. We're socialized to believe that there's a cap on the number of opportunities available to us and that other women are our competition.

The result?

These distracting, disempowering societal expectations have become something much more insidious. They've become the convincing scripts that sound out automatically in our heads and they masquerade as our own voice. The ultimate Trojan Horse, if you will.

Having these scripts programmed on auto play and sounding in our own voices is the reason we don't question them. It's the reason we believe the lies to be truths and it's the reason we continue playing smaller than what we're capable of and why we keep getting in the way of our own success.

When I realized this - that my limitations weren't actually MY limitations - my head pretty much exploded. I started to see how my confidence, my aspirations, my output and my potential were being unnecessarily tethered.

When I started to understand just how deeply embedded and pervasive these limiting scripts are in the lives of women I was overcome by the desire to rebel against them... and that's when I started using the phrase "Flip the Script".

To me, Flipping the Script means bucking the status quo; it means flipping a giant middle finger to conventional expectations; it means getting real with ourselves and turning the tables on the personal thought and behavior patterns that have been holding us back.

Flip the Script is a phrase I use to remind myself and my students that as women:

> We hold the power to be, do and have what we really want for our lives and careers

> We hold the power to do things that SERVE US

> We hold the power to things IN WAYS THAT SERVE US

> We hold the power to do things FOR REASONS THAT SERVE US.

It's a phrase I use to remind women that we hold the power to play our OWN game, by our OWN rules.

It's a reminder that all of those limiting conventions, expectations, beliefs and habits don't actually hold any truth; just as it was possible for us to adopt them in the first place, it's possible for us to ditch and replace them with new scripts that empower and propel us instead of suppress us.

The takeaway? Your ability to 'flip the script' is inextricably linked to your capacity to sustain consistent, high powered performance.

The 4 Pillars of High Powered Performance

Once I understood the root of my hang ups and how to flip the script on them, I was able to cut through the overwhelm and pinpoint the exact areas that I needed to master in order to sustain the kind of consistent, meaningful output that would help me take my game to the next level:

Energy

Clarity

Confidence

Systems and Support

Next, I set out to develop a rinse-and-repeat approach that comprised the tools, tactics and strategies that would make mastering these areas possible. Ample research, application and adaptation resulted in the categorical roadmap that in my mind, comprises the foundational elements that fuel high powered performance for women and enable us to live fiercely (and intentionally) true to our potential: The 4 Pillars of High Powered Performance.

These 4 Pillars are what helped me evolve on a very personal level so that I could finally answer that inner nudge to go beyond what I could do and start doing what I'm meant to do.

As mentioned earlier, they're the manual I still personally use as I continue to level-up and capitalize on my potential and they're the strategic approach I guide my students through as they master high powered performance for themselves.

I've included a description of each pillar below so that you can start identifying where your performance leaks are and what you need to focus on in order to mitigate them. Additionally, I've included an actionable tip with each pillar to help you flip the script and boost your high performance super powers right away.

The Catalyst - Fuel Your Engine

This is the match AND the gasoline. The Catalyst kickstarts and continues to fuel your progress through the other pillars and daily high powered performance by providing you with energy, physical strength, mental grit, mood and brain optimization, momentum and confidence.

Coach Rhi's HPP Tip:

Women have been socialized to misuse both fitness and food in restrictive, disempowering ways that actually limit our output - not optimize it. A tactic that's completely transformed my relationship with myself and my ability to show up as a high powered performer is to Flip the Script on diet culture and the expectation that women should be exercising and eating for the purpose of shrinking themselves. There is so much more to a woman and her body than a pant size or a number on the scale.

Rather than exercising and eating to lose weight, flip the script and start using fitness and nutrition in ways that energize you, that make you feel strong and powerful, that leave you feeling good and that remind you of what you're truly capable of - both physically and mentally.

The Compass - Align with Your Purpose for Power

This is highly personal, profound and powerful. The Compass is what guides you; it provides you with meaning, direction, strategy and drive. It's what helps you avoid distractions, overwhelm and burnout by enabling you to focus your resources on the things that really matter AND really move the needle.

Coach Rhi's HPP Tip:

Women have been socialized to doubt themselves, to seek external validation and to go with the flow. Because of this, we focus our resources on things that aren't truly meaningful to us and as a result, we end up unmotivated, unfulfilled and unsuccessful. A tactic that's enabled me to sustain focus, motivation and meaning is to Flip the Script on the expectation that women should seek purpose and approval from external sources by putting my blinders on and blocking out the noise so that I'm able to actually hear - and then focus on - my own voice and desires. Learning to trust and believe in ourselves is one of the most powerful skills we, as women, can acquire.

The Cohort - Draft Your MVPs

This is where you form the strong female relationships that translate into tangible empowerment. The Cohort is what amplifies you; it provides you with solidarity, strength and confidence. It's what helps you to be courageous and resilient so you can do and say what you need to fulfil your potential.

Coach Rhi's HPP Tip:

Women have been duped into thinking that other women pose a threat; that there aren't enough opportunities, partners or pieces of the proverbial pie to go around. We've been socialized to believe that another woman's success equates to our own missed opportunity or failure so we shy away from forming powerful, meaningful bonds with each other. A tactic that's helped me overcome self-doubt, find inspiration, empowerment and solidarity when I need it the most is to Flip the Script on the idea that I should be threatened or intimidated by ambitious, self-making women by purposely seeking them out, connecting with them and 'drafting' them to my very own team of MVP's who are by my side as I execute my world takeover strategy.

The Conveyor - Implement Your Personal Success Systems

This is where you craft the practice of limitless self-propulsion with systems designed to make success both sustainable and scalable. The Conveyor is what moves you toward your purpose and goals; it's the formation and practice of the rituals that compound to change your trajectory and change your life.

Coach Rhi's HPP Tip:

Too many women abandon the well thought out rituals and routines that sustain them and enable them to scale their success (and actually feel good about it!). This is because women (especially go-getters like you) are both inclined to take on 'all the things' at once and socialized to drop our own needs and priorities for those of others.

Two (#bonusround) tactics I use to help me avoid overwhelm, burnout and resentment so that I can be effective, happy and successful are:

1) To Flip the Script on my tendency to overload myself by exercising constraint and remembering that just because I can do something, doesn't mean I should. This forces me to choose and dedicate my resources to the things that will have the greatest impact on my success and in turn, frees up the bandwidth I need for sustained, high powered output.

2) To Flip the Script on the idea that 'Selfish' is bad by viewing my self-care, my work and any of the other personal success systems I've created in the same vein as putting the plane's oxygen mask on my face before helping anyone else with theirs. This reminds me that not only is it ok to put myself and my needs first, but that it's utterly necessary if I'm going to be able to show up consistently and effectively for myself or anyone else.

Now that you know how to flip the script on your limitations and what the foundational elements of High Powered Performance for women are, I hope you're feeling empowered to implement these concepts, to smash past your limits and to start living fiercely and intentionally true to your potential.

If you want to learn more or need a little extra help overcoming the hang-ups and performance blockers that have been keeping your game small, head over to: coachrhi.com/HPPquiz to take the high powered performance assessment that will help you identify where your super powers are and where you need to focus your efforts to really start kicking ass

Or email me at TheCoachRhi@gmail.com to set up a complimentary strategy session

ABOUT RHIANNON TARRANT

Seer of Potential, Smasher of Limits. Rhiannon Tarrant (aka, Coach Rhi) is a former corporate gal and athlete turned certified life coach, pro personal trainer and entrepreneur with an addiction to self-development and a mission to help women take over the world.

A success specialist for ambitious, self-making women looking to start playing BIG, Coach Rhi wants to help you flip the script on whatever's been holding you back from taking your game to the NEXT LEVEL; to make sure that you never have to settle for ordinary, mediocre or status quo; to help you get your sh*t together, stop spinning your wheels, stop stressing and FINALLY start doing the BADASS things you know you CAN - and SHOULD - be doing.

Beyond her passion for potential, Rhiannon loves being a pug mom to Frank and Mini, finding creative ways to stay active and jetting off to oceanside destinations with her favorite people.

RHIANNON TARRANT

PEPPER MAKEPEACE

HOW NOT TO FEEL ALONE IN YOUR BUSINESS

Any successful business involves a lot of people - fans, followers, customers, team members, designers, virtual assistants, editors, service providers, coaches, and more. But even with all of those people around, it's easy to feel alone and isolated inside your business.

Being part of a community of supportive, like-minded entrepreneurs has enormous benefits not only to the success of your business but also to your personal well-being.

I founded the Small Business Sisterhood in 2016 to support budding female entrepreneurs in a way that was sorely lacking when I first started my online business in 2008. I didn't have the safe space full of like-minded female entrepreneurs where I could make important business connections, get feedback on ideas, celebrate successes, and feel supported and cheered on. Trying to build a business without a community of peers is incredibly difficult and not a lot of fun. It's a miracle I didn't give up on my dreams completely.

Building my business alone in those early years involved a lot of starts and stops and more than a few frustrated tears. Many friends and family tried to be supportive and engaged in the process, but building a business online is different from working in a 9-5 job so it was difficult for them to relate. I tried a lot of local networking groups, but they mostly revolved around people wanting referrals or signups. Over time and through a lot of trial and error, I pieced together a group of like-minded folks that became my 'people'. Having my own community has had a huge impact on how I feel about my business and my place in the online business world.

We Are Stronger Together

Thankfully, the concept of community has been shifting in the online business industry in recent years, especially among women business owners. More and more entrepreneurs are seeing the tremendous benefit of community. More communities are forming that support growth, nurture collaboration, favor connection over competition, and allow for deeper, long-lasting #bizbestie relationships that support you and your business beyond just getting referrals.

Seeing your fellow entrepreneurs as members of your community, and not as competition, can have a profound impact on how you serve your clients and customers. Even when on the surface your target audiences and services may look very similar, we each bring something entirely unique to our businesses – ourselves! No one can run a business exactly like you do. Seeing the immense value in your own uniqueness and the uniqueness of others is empowering and makes us all stronger.

Here are just a few of the benefits of community:

Feedback

It's easy to get stuck in our heads wasting time and holding ourselves back. Having a second set of eyes and ears to work through things and consider factors you hadn't even thought of is invaluable and can save you time, money, and heartache. Your community is a great place to get feedback on all aspects of your business such as your ideas for a new product, your onboarding process, your website sales page, or even challenging clients.

Accountability

When you're the boss and the enforcer of deadlines, it can be easy to let things wait until next week. It's not like you're going to get fired, right? But setting and keeping goals is critical for keeping the needle moving forward in your business. Your community is a great place to find some accountability, both for working on stuff and taking care of yourself.

One of my favorite activities in the Small Business Sisterhood is our virtual coworking. It amazes me how much I can get done in half an hour when I know I have to report what I accomplished when reconvened for a break. It really keeps me focused and aware of how I'm spending my time. Keeping each other on track and working on what matters most helps me accomplish a lot in a short amount of time.

Emotional Support

If you've been an entrepreneur for any length of time, I'm sure you're aware of the emotional roller coaster that comes with the territory. Feeling understood and supported as a business owner goes a long way to balance the stress that comes with building and running a business. Having a safe space to talk about the successes and struggles of entrepreneur life is a powerful benefit of having a business community you trust and can lean on.

While an emotional support system may not be a sexy topic that boosts your revenue, it just might save your life. You don't have to think very hard to come up with a name of a talented and successful entrepreneur we've tragically lost to suicide – Kate Spade, Anthony Bourdain, Aaron Schwartz, and sadly so many more. In their article "Depression Among Entrepreneurs is an Epidemic Nobody is Talking About", The Hustle states, "Riding the entrepreneurial roller coaster can cause depression, but refusing to talk about it will make it worse." In fact, studies have shown that entrepreneurs are twice as likely to suffer from depression, a major cause of suicide. Being able to lean on people who can relate to the highs and lows of entrepreneurship is a crucial aspect of mental health as business owners.

But even if you don't suffer from depression, a supportive community can help you process and overcome any level of stress or isolation you might be feeling in your business. Reach out to your community for support. You are not alone!

Buzz for Your Biz

Community can also be a great way to boost your bottom line. Your community can help you reach new audiences and expand your offerings. Whether it's collaborating on projects and events or cross-promoting each other's latest program launch – community helps create a lot of buzz around your business that would otherwise be hard to come by when you're going it alone. This adds to your impact and your income.

Inspiration

It is so inspiring to see others in our community being brave, breaking through challenges, asking for what they deserve, being resilient, helping others succeed. Their success becomes fuel for our fire, motivating us to reach higher and be braver. Then we, in turn, inspire others to do the same. What a beautiful cycle of lifting each other up! Cultivating around us an environment of encouragement and inspiration is so much more empowering than seeing others as competition. I choose to be inspired!

Giving Back

It's not just what you GET out of your community, it's also what you GIVE. It's an amazing feeling to know your community has your back. Reciprocating the support and being there for members of your community is also an incredibly rewarding experience. Many of us became business owners because we are driven to serve and have a life of purpose. Giving back to your business community is certainly aligned with those values. We are all stronger for it!

Surely by now you're sold on the idea of community. But now you're wondering what to do about it. How do you find a community that fits you?

Here are 3 Steps to Get You Started Building Your Community:

1. Coffee

Have virtual coffee with folks you know online. Reach out and have a chat on Skype or Zoom. This is the easiest and quickest way to get started. Just a simple message to say "I'd love to learn more about you and your business. Fancy a virtual coffee?" is all you need to do.

Have in-person coffee with fellow entrepreneurs. Pick a small business owner in your area that you admire or think you might click with and reach out to them. Be upfront that your intention is just getting to know them better and not trying to make a sale. Heading to an event or conference? Choose one or two people to meet with again one-on-one over coffee.

2. Online Memberships

Online membership groups come in different shapes and sizes and with a variety of purposes. Some focus on learning. While others are purely social. Some are a mix. You're sure to find one that fits you and your needs. Try them out and then stick with the one that suits you best. Just remember you get what you give, so engage and participate to the best of your ability and capacity.

Be sure to include the Small Business Sisterhood in your options! We'd love to have you. Check us out at SmallBusinessSisterhood.com.

3. Networking with Intention

Networking groups certainly have their place in any healthy marketing strategy. Many of the local networking groups I have participated in have been geared towards presenting your elevator pitch and hoping someone gives a shit about what you're offering. You don't have to be a part of yucky make-a-sale type networking groups but finding a group you love that offers a supportive community will take some trial and error. When you're evaluating groups, pay attention to how you feel when you interact with other members and how you feel about what's expected of you. Some groups are just weird. [It's not you. It's them.] Other groups are structured in ways that may not suit your personality. You'll have to experiment a little bit and see what works best for you. As an introvert, I prefer groups where I don't have to stand up in front of a large group and give a 30-second pitch. But that's not to say that someone else wouldn't thrive in situations that make them nauseous. Find out what you like and do more of that!

Now that you know all the amazing benefits of community, I hope you'll be inspired to take action and find 'your people' so you can start reaping those benefits for yourself and your business. Include your community as part of your regular business routine. It will make you AND your business stronger and more successful and give you the resilience you need when things get tough.

Get started with your FREE membership to the Small Business Sisterhood, https://smallbusinesssisterhood.com - a community tailor-made for entrepreneurs like you - solopreneurs, side hustlers, new business owners. It's crafted to support you, help you stay focused, motivated, and accountable, and get stuff done in your business so it can grow and thrive.

ABOUT PEPPER MAKEPEACE

Pepper firmly believes that entrepreneurship is not for the faint of heart and anyone brave enough to give it a go is cool as shit in her book. She loves supporting female business owners with branding, web design, and online business strategy at www.peppermakepeace.com. As an online business owner since 2008, Pepper has quite the library of tools and strategy secrets stored up in her brain and on her hard drive.

Even more important is her understanding of the emotional ups and downs and mental games that come with building a business. Her passion project is the Small Business Sisterhood smallbusinesssisterhood.com - an online community of like-minded women growing their businesses and supporting each other along the way. It's one thing to have the strategy. And it's another to have incredible emotional support along the journey. That's where the soul of the Small Business Sisterhood shines - the connection and community spirit that lift us all.

PEPPER MAKEPEACE

SAMANTHA POPP

YOU ARE ENOUGH. YOU'VE ALWAYS BEEN ENOUGH.

I used to have ZERO self-confidence and to be totally honest, the whole self-belief thing wasn't something I understood let alone had. I remember feeling anxious, frustrated, and worried about WHERE my life was heading. It was as though I was a passenger in my own car, someone else was driving and I was just along for the ride.

I struggled with an eating disorder, ended up in abusive relationships and had NO idea HOW to get myself the hell out of dodge. My confidence played a HUGE role in my ability to leave and or belief that I could.

One thing I learnt was that for far too long I remained a victim of my own reality. I continuously made a CHOICE to stay in both of my abusive relationships for far too long because I was mentality stuck in a rut. I had to learn how to flex my confidence muscle...and once I got that cased I never looked back. I started to INTENTIONALLY build a beautiful fucking life for myself and if no one has told you this yet, YOU CAN TOO!

So, if you're feeling down with all of these dreams with no direction and feel like you're lacking self-confidence? I feel you and I got you babe.

Being confident doesn't appear out of nowhere! I had to make the conscious decision that I AM WORTHY and that I deserve all the good this life has in store for me. You're probably wondering how I gained my self-confidence and how I learned to love ALL parts of myself...I'm happy to say that I'm going to walk you through my 5 step process that will help you build confidence, radiate self-love and live authentic as fuck! If I can, YOU CAN!

1 HOW TO ATTRACT WHAT YOU DESIRE

Your thoughts have a much bigger impact than you sometimes give them credit for.

You know, I've always wondered why we seem to be so damn hard on ourselves. Hear me out...If you believe that you always attract negativity into your life, then to be honest that's exactly what you're inviting in. For example: you constantly feel like you can't call in the love of your life, or an incredible career opportunity, or you don't seem to have the courage/motivation to achieve your goals. So, my question for you is: If you constantly think you CAN'T...what continues to happen? How does this way of thinking leave you feeling at the end of the day?

Since a very young age, it's been engraved in our minds that we MUST work hard for what we want and if we don't...for some reason we won't get it, because that makes total sense...NOT! We were taught to suppress our emotions...that what we were/are feeling is somehow invalid...and as we continue to grow older and older everyone and their dog has been trying to tell us WHO we should be, WHAT we should be doing and WHERE we should be going. That type of environment doesn't leave you with the opportunity for much personal growth. But here you are, making a choice that YOU deserve more and are capable of achieving that.

If someone hasn't told you this yet, I'm proud to be the first...YOU, YES YOU ARE AMAZING exactly as you are! Everything about you is beautiful and NO ONE and I mean NO ONE can tell you who you should or shouldn't be. YOU HOLD THIS POWER WITHIN.

Take some time to think about what you want in your life and what it looks like for you. Imagine it's five years from today. What does your life look like? What have you accomplished? What goals did you set for yourself and achieve? When you start imagining your future and truly thinking about everything you want...you can start making decisions NOW that will impact your journey moving forward.

2 TREAT YOURSELF RIGHT

"How you treat yourself sets the tone for how others will treat you."

Here's an exercise I'd like you to try. What you'll need is - a journal, a pen, a mirror and you.

When you stand in-front of the mirror, who's the woman staring back at you...what do you see? How does she feel about her current reality? How does she feel about herself? What does she see? Do you see a strong resilient woman that will do whatever it takes? Or do you feel stressed, worried and frustrated? Take a moment and journal this out.

I want you to pay attention to both the negative and the positive thoughts you've written down.

Any negative, mean, or rude comments you've written down about yourself, cross those out and replace them with 2-3 positive things you know about yourself without a doubt are TRUE. This starts to rewire our brain and shift into gratitude and appreciation for yourself in the now!

Looking at your list, how does this make you feel? If it's through journaling or talking aloud, do what feels good and something that will encourage you to express your thoughts and emotions throughout this exercise.

Now, onto the next step - take a moment and think, if you had everything you've ever dreamed of, how would you feel? Does this woman give herself a pep talk every damn day? Does she give herself credit for all of her hard work? Does she speak HIGHLY of herself? That's what you need to figure out, BUT one thing that is an absolute non-negotiable at this point is that it's time to speak to yourself with kindness, love and understanding. The moment you start treating yourself this way, you begin to build a solid foundation towards your journey of continuous self-love and growth.

3 KNOW WHAT (ACTUALLY) MAKES *YOU* HAPPY?

What is it that you really want? For this next step, I encourage you to take a couple of days off of social media or whatever it is that seems to impact your decisions. I want you to tune into your mind and get rid of all that exterior noise. What's the ONE thing that keeps you up at night? I like to call it.. "The fire in your belly." Really dive deep and figure it out - Is it to travel the world? To climb a mountain, become an entrepreneur or maybe purchase your own house? Whatever that ONE thing may be...if it keeps coming up...acknowledge it and listen to what it's trying to tell you because it's coming up for a reason.

Once you figure out what your "fire" is, this is when it's time to "do the damn thing!" You deserve a full and happy life. In order to achieve that, it's up to you to start making choices, and DOING the things you LOVE to do! I call this - TAKING ACTION AND OWNING IT!

Here's a pro tip I wish I knew when I was going through my very own transformation: once you plan or do your thing, be mindful that others may have an opinion that differs from yours. They may choose to tell you how they feel and here's where you come in...put those blinders on baby and DO WHAT MAKES YOU HAPPY no matter what other people think, do or say. It's so much fun once you start living your life for you instead of others.

4 SHOUT IT FROM THE ROOFTOP BABY!

This is one of the most important tips I can give you: USE YOUR VOICE BECAUSE YOUR VOICE MATTERS. You may not realize it yet, but your voice really does matter and can make a BIG difference in your life and maybe even someone else's life. That's for damn sure! You need to speak your mind and ask for what you want, because if you don't, we all know the quote "If you don't ask, the answer will always be no."

Ever get stuck in your head thinking about all the ways someone MIGHT respond to your question. Thinking about all the ways the situation might play out?! I feel we've all done this at some point or another. If you want something or need something, no matter what - ask for it. As my teacher used to tell me: "There are no silly questions!"

Using your voice is such a powerful tool. No one can read your mind, so how are they going to know what you want? Simple answer: they can't. A solution is to speak up for what you want and ask the questions you need answers to.

Pro tip: give yourself a quick pep talk before these conversations to ensure you're confident going into them. Stand in your power, always. YOU GOT THIS!

5 KEEP ON KEEPIN' ON

Never give up on yourself because you are the best project you can ever work on! You are the one that's creating your future. Yes, YOU! Not anyone else! People can try to tell you how to live your life, but you have the final say in what actually happens. You get to make the decisions. You're running the show. NEVER FORGET IT!

Here's the thing, I would not be the person I am today without the mistakes I've made. As you continue on your journey of self-love and confidence you'll begin to understand that your mistakes are what mold into your successes. We learn from our mistakes. Mistakes give us an opportunity to try again! It gives you an opportunity to evaluate what went wrong and even what went right! Learn from your mistakes and implement new lessons. Start creating the life you want. "It's yours for the taking."

BONUS TIP: GLOW UP GIRL!

You have the power to step into your higher self and that time is NOW! Yes, YOU, I'm talking to you - You can do it! You can build your confidence by becoming aware of one of the BIGGEST things…WHO YOU ARE! For a moment think about who you are outside of how others may define you or even how you've defined yourself. This will help you dig deeper into the amazing being you already are.

The choice is yours. It's never too late to start. It's time to embrace yourself 100%. It's all up to you, but in case you need permission from someone, here it is - I give you permission to do the damn thing, to go after your dreams and to tune into who you truly are, because you deserve the best possible life.

I'd love to help you on this journey inside my FREE community on Facebook: "There She Glows". The group exists to help you step into your purpose, nurture your relationship, prioritize yourself and quell your inner critic to create a life you're wildly obsessed with!

I believe in you and I'm sending you all the love!

ABOUT SAMANTHA POPP

Samantha is a Relationship & Sex Expert who helps women re-ignite their honeymoon phase so they can experience passion, fulfilment, and THE BEST SEX LIFE EVER!

She's a dog mama to her rescue Twister, girlfriend to the love of her life, author and PROUD AF entrepreneur.

Sam is the FOUNDER of the women's empowerment group There She Glows, Creator of The Glow Girl Method and Host of the blog Glow The Fuck Up.

Samantha believes that making yourself a priority is the first step to creating both a life and a relationship with your partner that you're wildly obsessed with. You can have it all.

CONCLUSION

CONCLUSION

Thank you so much for reading our book!

Our greatest hope is that we have inspired and motivated you to intentionally create success rituals to support your goals and dreams.

Feel free to borrow one of ours! That's why we've shared our winning habits with you.

Successful women realize they possess the ability to influence their success. They are highly conscious of their thoughts and actions, and they choose to move forward consistently with a strong sense of purpose.

As you develop your own winning habits, you can slide into the driver's seat of your success too!

Sending you love and wishing you good fortune,

The Success Rituals V2 Co-Author Crew

CONCLUSION

SHARE THE LOVE

The co-author crew would love your help to get this book into the hands of aspiring women entrepreneurs around the globe.

Here are three simple things you can do, and we thank you in advance…

- Post a review on Amazon.
- Share what you love most about the book on social media using #thesuccessrituals.
- Recommend it to a friend.

Please remember to take full advantage of the free resources provided by the co-authors. We are here to elevate your success.

Gina Raelene,

Publisher and CEO, Victress Press